William E. Edwards

TEN DAYS

TO A GREAT

NEW LIFE

Foreword by Melvin Powers

Cover photograph

TIRZA & MELVIN POWERS

1977 EDITION

Published by
Melvin Powers
WILSHIRE BOOK COMPANY
12015 Sherman Road
No. Hollywood, California 91605
Telephone: (213) 875-1711

Fifth Printing . . . . *May, 1965*

Wilshire Book Company edition
is published by special arrangement
with Prentice-Hall, Inc., Englewood Cliffs, N. J.

Printed by

HAL LEIGHTON PRINTING CO.
P.O. Box 1231
Beverly Hills, California 90213
Telephone: (213) 983-1105

ISBN 0-87980-159-X

FOREWORD

As more and more of the always controversial postulations of Sigmund Freud (1856-1939) are cast in further doubt by continuing psychological investigation, it is clear that contemporary psychiatrists are no longer satisfied with a statistical rate of cure that is no better than that of mentally or emotionally disturbed individuals who receive no treatment at all.

The main goal of an increasing number of psychotherapists today is to utilize anything that will induce quick improvement in patients whether the agent is a tranquilizer, group therapy or a blending of psycho-physiological techniques which offer comparatively rapid improvement as compared with time-consuming psychoanalytic measures. This search for faster methods of relieving incapacitating neuroses and psychoses is necessary because psychiatrists and hospital beds are in short supply, prohibitively expensive, and the advent of Medicare patients will increase the load on present facilities beyond their capacity.

This hunt for a more effective method to return the mentally and emotionally ill to everyday life has had its counterpart in the testing of many techniques to relieve the anxiety and tensions of countless individuals who never become incapacitated, but whose inability to achieve the goals they seek leads to widespread frustration and unhappiness. Very few people, it would appear from polls, are satisfied with their efforts to attain success or contentment in our cybernated society.

There is, of course, an estrangement or feeling of dislocation which afflicts us all in these parlous times, but I am not speaking of these side effects that accompany what has been called "The Age of Anxiety," or the fears attendant on labels referring to the increasing danger of nuclear disaster, either by accident or design. I am speaking, rather, of the devastating effects of the failure of so many people to find their hoped for niche in our complicated society. The fulfillment of the American dream is becoming ever more difficult as depersonalized computers replace man.

The sale of books on self-improvement indicates that millions of Americans who will never become psychiatric patients yearn for recognition of what talents they feel they possess, and yet their employment records indicate they have no specialized talents, in most cases, equal to machines which instantaneously answer questions in a minute which formerly required hours or days. This is a cruel blow to our egos even though the facade we present to others shows no hint of our inner hurt or turmoil. We have mastered the art of masking our emotions, and even take spurious pride in maintaining the stiff upper lip so prized by British citizens no matter what their station in life.

The emergence of Self-Image psychology has helped many individuals to attain goals which would have been beyond their reach if they had not sought the education or its equivalent which was necessary to their realization, but it is impossible to estimate the number of people who dreamed of goals inconsistent with their talents—and then gave up because of the time involved in making them come true. This is the real modern tragedy.

Time takes on a special significance in this context, and for that reason William E. Edwards has written this much needed and important book. It is his theory—and many have proved it—that an individual can change the direction of his whole life in 10 days by a few simple actions. Faced with inhuman competition, this is important for him if he is to retain his identity and self-respect.

Mr. Edwards is a practical man, and he makes it clear that the average person wants something to happen quickly after he has chosen a goal. Very few would quarrel with that thesis. He makes it equally clear that even long range goals must produce some almost immediate results or the dream is likely to be extinguished. Very few would honestly argue with that premise either.

This common sense attitude about goals and the possibility of their achievement goes back to the first extensive research in Self-Image psychology done by the late Prescott Lecky. In his book, *Self-Consistency,* he counselled that one's goals must always be consistent with one's abilities, but allowed room for latitude by stating that each individual must *define for himself the nature of that totality which he is.*

It is as natural for some individuals to overestimate their abilities as it is for some to conclude they are inferior, and this book provides both solace and hope to those who have nurtured impossible goals. It is true that any American boy may become President of the United States, but it is equally true that most of them will not.

It is quite probable, in reading of the power embodied in Self-Image psychology, that many persons set their goals so high that they cannot even take the first faltering steps toward their realization. This is unfortunate because human beings are so constituted that they must have some tangible results from their efforts rapidly or they will lose hope.

This book, then, is written for those who want to change the course of their life—fast. It is for those who want to get out of the rut—now. Each chapter has sample charts which measure the simple actions recommended against the results.

There is no lack of books relating to the long, hard road to success which many individuals have followed. The American saga of rags to riches is well known, but what is not so well known, Mr. Edwards believes, is that the road does not *have* to be *that* long or hard.

The fact is that many young men these days are creating exciting and rewarding careers for themselves while others merely mark time, waiting for the man ahead to move up and make room for them. There is no rule that says success must be achieved in this way, but too many young men overlook present opportunities as they peer dimly and fearfully into the future.

Here is a book, if you will give its contents a fair trial, that will force those who look hopefully to the future to look at the present. It is the only book I know of that allows no procrastination. You choose your goals and you start achieving them as fast as you can get a pen and paper. If that sounds like hyperbole, try it anyway. After all, the chances are better than even that you are reading this book because of some self-doubt.

Any system of self-improvement that offers the added incentive of speedy reward deserves at least a trial, but in this case I am happy to add that you run no risk. Mr. Edwards has already used the techniques successfully on thousands of men and women, and the outcome has been notably outstanding. There is no reason why you should be an exception unless you persist in negative thinking that has probably brought you to this point of seeking improvement.

I pretend no understanding of why Mr. Edwards' system works as well as it does other than to point out that audio-visual techniques are becoming more and more useful in education. Some students, it has been established, learn more easily by listening (lecture courses, for example) than by reading, and the converse is also true. Mr. Edwards has found that the simple task of writing down one's goals and referring to them frequently is a powerful aid in realizing those goals "in the back of your head."

Knowing this, it seems to me that a combination of the two methods seems the most efficacious way of hastening one's ambitions to fruition.

Certainly this book is for those who need a constant reminder of what they must do to accomplish their desires, just as there are a large number of students who must supplement lectures and discussions with notes and industrious trips to the library.

It is extremely fortunate that these individuals are Mr. Edwards' chief concern, for they are in the majority. Few people have the gift of total recall or can invariably resist procrastination when pleasure calls.

As a penultimate conclusion, it can be said that Dr. Maxwell Maltz has written a book[1] on Self-Image psychology for those who have no difficulty in remembering every detail of consecration their goals require, whereas Mr. Edwards has written a book for those who must daily reinfuse themselves with their own written promises to keep their dreams alive, lest they become laggards.

All in all, it is a not unhappy situation because every person knows the fashion in which he functions best, or at least he will after experimenting for a time.

With this sort of available help, there is no reason for anyone to be a failure, and I wish you luck in anything that is your heart's desire. Furthermore, I do it confidently because I know unfailing help is available. You have only to make the decision concerning what sort of help you need, and if you are honest and reasonably objective this decision should not be too difficult.

Good luck, then, and best wishes, but in truth you cannot fail if you sincerely wish to succeed. It is extremely important to bear this in mind, and banish negative thoughts. They are your only bar to every goal that is consistent with your potential abilities. Feelings of inferiority plague almost everyone, high or low. Remember that and take heart.

As a final bit of advice it might be well to remember Shakespeare's paraphrased advice that if you are honest with yourself you cannot be false to any man. This becomes important when you recall that honesty, other factors being equal, pays off more than any other virtue in the long run, contrary to anything would-be cynics may say.

This foreword is longer than I had envisioned, but a man who is happiest inspiring his fellowman to live up to the best that is in him sometimes exceeds what he had originally planned to say, and so, once more, I wish you everything you

[1] *Psycho-Cybernetics*, Maxwell Maltz, Wilshire Book Company, 1963

have the imagination to realistically conceive as goals.

Mr. Edwards' book will be of great benefit in your efforts. Follow his advice with exactitude. The results will surprise you. I confess they surprised me, for the simplicity of his techniques seemed unglamorous compared to those employed by most self-improvement books.

Mr. Edwards' methods, however, have one virtue lacking in many books with similar objectives. They work. And if I may be permitted an old fashioned expression, the proof of the pudding is still in the eating.

Why not start your new diet today?

Melvin Powers

12015 Sherman Road
No. Hollywood, California 91605

Contents

Here's the technique. How the man with "pad and points" dominated a conference. The man who wouldn't make a phone call without it. The "pad and points" works wonders with your boss. And the boss himself should use this technique. One of America's selling giants calls it a miracle. No place is too small for this technique. This technique can change you in ten days. Blueprint-for-action section.

Here's the technique. Here's the exciting background story. The young matron who wanted social success. You can use this dynamite no matter where you are—no matter what your job. "Talent show-through and follow-up" enabled me to write a million-dollar letter. Management gets into the act. The young man who thought he wanted to be a banker. His old friend straightens him out. Self-reliance means something more than belief in your ability to handle things. Stop crawling and start flying. Blueprint-for-action section.

PART III
HOW TO UNLEASH YOUR FULL MENTAL POWERS

Here's the technique. Your unlimited idea potential. The simple technique that primes the pump. A department head makes up a list. These lists are terrific time bombs. The list that yielded a jackpot idea three weeks later. This technique enables you to spot ideas from the ordinary things that surround you. Don't make this costly mistake. Women can use this technique in dozens of ways. Don't make your lists too long. Specific examples of success. Blueprint-for-action section.

Here's the technique. There are two rules to follow. Why this is one of the hottest techniques a person can use. But great as that is—you'll get a second benefit that seems nothing short of a miracle. The young man who woke up his life with a "scrapbook." The young man speaks up. The car pool defers to him. But you've got to clip

Action 2 To supply you with exciting new information you can use with breath-taking power *(continued)*

and paste. Use this technique now. The young lady was scornful of the scrapbook idea. What happens when you feed them to your scrapbook? Many great persons have used this technique. What a scrapbook did for me. The scrapbook is mental capital. Your own idea of yourself. Who should keep a scrapbook? A general—or a special—scrapbook? I've started my scrapbook again. Great men and fools. What to do. Blueprint-for-action section.

Here's the technique. What do we mean by forming judgments? He should turn at once to this "list of factors" technique. Instances of where to use this technique. The young man with weak judgment. One reason we hate to think. How this list of factors "outsmarts" the mind. This technique gives a "non-thinker" judgment. This technique gives a person courage to make decisions. Touching all bases. The list of factors technique pushes through decisions that are ready to be made. Improve your judgment. It's the path to strength. This technique is a powerhouse. Blueprint-for-action section.

PART IV
HOW TO INCREASE YOUR WEALTH

Here's the technique. Immediate help through this technique. The $2,000 expense. The decision pays off fast. Where do you eat lunch and with whom? Hobbies or a career. The unhappy fisherman. And what about your evenings? Here's where this technique comes in. Drive drives out the fear of failure. Blueprint-for-action section.

Here's the technique. A little ice cream store hits the jackpot. The young fellow who was going to get $10,000 a year or quit. But this law works both ways. Here's a good example. A sound foundation for positive thinking. This formula turned the tide for me. The insurance man who refused to write a $10,000 policy. It works everywhere. When business serves it will prosper. A top example of this law at work. But why won't we learn this lesson? You have three choices—but you must take one. Blueprint-for-action section.

Action 3 To improve your circumstances rapidly—no matter what they are (*continued*)

cided to stay. Relief in a matter of hours. So what do I have to lose? Bill wakes up. Bill solves his problem. Maybe you don't need to change jobs. Mildred likes Emerson. Mildred maps out a plan. And she got some hot new ideas. Maybe it won't work the same way for you—but it will work. Fred does an about face—skyrockets from failure to success. Fred was trying to duck reality. But my set-up is terrible. Fred is reluctant—but he tries. Fred gets three tremendous benefits right off the bat. We're not talking about "adjustment." Blueprint-for-action section.

How fast does this program really work? These actions work for everybody. This is a desk manual for living—not a book to be read once. In what order shall I take on these actions? The utter realism of this book. Life is meant to be an ecstasy. You've got to get living. What do you want? The program is complete—all worked out for you. What will it be for you? A large order? Begin your new life now.

Every man who knows how to read has it in his power to magnify himself, to multiply the ways in which he exists, to make his life full, significant and interesting.

—Aldous Huxley

A MIGHTY SEND-OFF

In the next ten days you can change your whole life

This book tells the story of a miracle that's waiting for every one of us. It shows how a few simple actions performed for ten days can change your whole life—how these actions throw open the floodgates of life—release your latent powers—make you a hundred times as effective in everything you do.

It doesn't matter how bad things may be going for you—how broke you may be—how frustrated you are—how much you're in the doghouse with everyone. These actions can change things fast. They're different from all other actions. As soon as you touch them they set off a psychological explosion. They have the special ability to release a thousand times the power it takes to perform them. But they do much more than give you new strength and energy—they give you strength *right where you need it,* the five kinds of superiorities that make for a victorious life. Here are the five great things these actions will do for you—and fast:

1. They'll set your life on fire with your real goals—goals that are your heart's desire—goals that integrate your special talents with your special kind of temperament—and they'll give you the energy, hope and enthusiasm for their fulfillment.

2. They'll give you a belief in yourself such as you've never known before—a belief so strong you'll tackle anything—be ready to deal with anyone; they'll give you a confidence that sweeps everything before it.

3. They'll multiply by ten the amount of mental powers that you use—give you "cerebration in depth." This will enable you to out-think others—to tower over them in judgment—to be a fountainhead of solid and brilliant ideas.

4. They'll open up to you the most powerful money principles in existence—powerful psychological principles that magically invest in the real you—that center everything on your special talents so your money-making, power-gaining capacities keep doubling back on themselves— are endlessly multiplied.

5. Greatest of all—no matter what your current set-up, no matter how thwarted your life may be—these actions will enable you to use your current "here and now" as your take-off point for a victorious life.

This specific-action-technique brings the promise of a great new day. If you don't like the way things are going for you—if you feel you have powers you have had no opportunity to express—if you want ten times the life you're now living, here is the high road to happiness, success and fulfillment.

These action-techniques work for anyone—anywhere

The special actions explained in this book work for everyone, everywhere. They work for men, they work for women. They work for executives, they work for housewives. They work their "magic" for professional people—for salesmen—for people who are employed by others—for people who run their own businesses. They are fundamental principles of action that can fit into anyone's life. They can be applied by anyone, anywhere to open up a great new life.

But first a word of warning

These actions are simple to take—but some people don't want to act at all. They'll do anything but take action. You *must* take these simple actions—and we've made it still simpler for you to take them. The whole thing is laid out like a blueprint—filled with helps that lead you right into the actions—make them almost automatic. You'll have the feeling that someone is working things out with you every step of the way. But remember this: as soon as you make the first move on any one of these actions it's like throwing a switch—enormous new power is released—power that carries the action along on its own.

The feature of this book— the thing that makes it a bombshell

Remember that this is no ordinary book. It delivers an explosive new formula for "specific actions for victorious living" that makes it terrific—but the one feature of this book that makes it a bombshell is the "Blueprint-for-Action" section at the end of each chapter. These sections consist of just a few pages each, but they're the heart of the whole business.

They enable you to take the electrifying action
—explained in the chapter—with almost automatic ease. They give you just the special kind
of help you need to put the action across in
your life with a bang.

Never has there been so exciting a book

Never has there been so exciting a program
for breaking your life wide open. It has everything.

What do you want? Do you want money
and success? Do you want recognition? Do you
want new self-assurance and confidence? Do
you want to multiply your mental effectiveness? Do you want to convert static goals into
great dynamos of energy within you? Do you
want to launch right out from things as they
are today and change them fast? Do you want
to live ten times the life you're now living?
This book is your answer.

Remember the one great theme of this book
—that only action can help you—that only action will do the trick. It doesn't matter how
much you *know* about confidence—and success
—and the rules for victorious living. Unless you
can take the action that throws the switch you
can change nothing. Here in this book are the
actions that throw the switch—the specific
actions that throw open the portals of life. The
only thing that can change your circumstances
—and change you—is action. Not action in gen-

eral—but specific actions. Here, all ready for you, are the miracles of action.

Let's go

Turn now to Part I—and let's start this exciting new venture into action by taking the action that sets your goals on fire. It's terrific.

HOW TO SET
YOUR GOALS ON FIRE

Part I of this book deals with a single great action—an action that breathes fire into your goals—sets them ablaze with power—turns your goals into humming dynamos that pour forth the energy, the hope, the enthusiasm for their own realization.

When one young man used this action he expressed his amazement this way—

I found my whole being suffused with an excited enthusiasm for my everyday business and surroundings. Before I took this action I had not even thought of my goals as being goals at all but as just some thoughts in my mind.

And then he added excitedly—

My goals now flood every minute of my life with meaning. This action pulled me right out of the rut I was in and put me on the high road to fulfillment.

Let's launch out on a great new life by taking this first great action—the first of a dozen electric actions given in this book for vibrant victorious living.

To set

your goals on fire

This first action breathes the fire of life into your goals and makes it possible for you to realize those goals faster than anything else in the world. And it's utterly simple to use.

Here's the technique:

No matter what you want to achieve—whether it's a great lifetime goal or some quick short objective—write it down—*get a statement of your goal on paper.*

That's all. That's the whole action. The small amount of effort it takes to get your goal on paper will be repaid to you 10,000 times over—and you'll start to be repaid at once. This is the most rewarding mechanism the human mind can use. No matter how things are going for you, this simple technique can change things virtually overnight, step up vigorously the tempo of your life, give you dynamic new force in everything you do.

This one act of getting down on paper a statement of your goals will do more for their realization than thinking and talking about them forever. But despite the wonder-working power of this action, not one person in a hundred ever uses it. If you want to lead a victorious life filled with happiness, success and fulfillment, start using this technique today and use it for everything you want to accomplish. It's dynamite.

How I discovered this dynamic principle by accident

Twenty years ago I wrote to a good friend of mine a letter in which I devoted one short paragraph to an idea I was then thinking about. Without knowing it I was writing down my goal—was getting a statement of my goal on paper. Here's the paragraph from the letter—

> I've been thinking lately about writing a course for young executives—a course that would cover the seven or eight hot pivotal points for executive success. I'd like to write such a course and sell it by mail —handle the whole operation myself. I'll write the advertising letter that sells the course. I'll have the courses printed up and ship them out as orders come in.

That was all I wrote about the matter—but writing down that one statement of my aim changed my life. Getting it down on paper gave substance to the thought.

It set the stage for changing it into a reality—which no amount of thinking about the project could ever have done. This was the act that planted the seed. (Getting the statement on paper was like getting the seed into the ground.)

How the project worked out

Did everything work out just as per the plan I described in the letter to my friend? No—not exactly—but it worked out very well for me. I wrote the course for young executives—and then I wrote the advertising letter to sell the course—and then I hit a snag. The cost of having the course printed was more than I could then afford.

But I didn't stop there. Thanks to having written down my goal, the project had gained momentum—and so had I. I called on a large publishing house that specialized in selling courses by mail. They were impressed with my work and offered me a job selling courses by mail for them. In a matter of months I was selling courses on a scale I had never dreamed possible. My income soared. My goal had not materialized exactly as I had written it down—but it *had* materialized—and with a vengeance. The point to remember is this: unless you write down a statement of what you want you're apt to get nothing—but when you write it down you're very apt to get something close to it— and often something bigger and better than the thing you had in mind.

This technique brings dramatic success for all kinds of goals

Ever since I discovered the magic there is in writing down my goals I've been using this technique everywhere in my work—but I had never applied it to personal things. I've now discovered that it works its magic just as well on personal projects as on vocational goals.

For years I had been some 30 pounds overweight and nothing I had been able to do would take off more than a couple of pounds—which I would soon regain. Once when I tried to run for a bus I got so winded that when I got into the bus the high school boys riding in it started laughing and singing out, "Thar she blows! Thar she blows!" I tried to smile it off, but I was doing anything but smiling inside. Right then and there I determined to get my weight down—and I tackled the problem with renewed force. I ate less and exercised more—but in about a week I saw the same old pattern emerging. I began to lose pep. I asked myself if it was really worthwhile. I told myself that I wasn't feeling too well, that I couldn't keep it up.

When I went for my annual physical checkup the doctor told me just what he had told me at every checkup— to get my weight down, and he gave me one of those little printed sheets that told me just what I should eat. I gave it a good try for a couple of days. It was the same story all over again. I told myself I couldn't keep it up.

Then I decided to try on weight reduction the technique that had been so phenomenally successful in my work goals. I wrote down the following—

> I want to get my weight down to 165 pounds and get
> in hard athletic trim. [And then I added] As soon as
> I hit 165 pounds I'll buy myself a black pull-over
> sweater and a pair of slacks.

Adding that line about the sweater and the slacks was a sudden inspiration (based on an ad I had seen in the *New Yorker* magazine). I know how silly this sounds—but the things that move us to action are not always appeals to our logic. It helped me dramatize the value of getting my weight down. I pictured myself looking like the gent in the *New Yorker* ad (which shows I have imagination, if nothing else)—and the sweater and the slacks were to be my reward for achieving success. *But the main thing was— I had gotten my goal down on paper.*

And it worked like a charm. In four months I had achieved my goal. I didn't look exactly like the fellow in the *New Yorker* ad—but I was mighty pleased with the result. This was years ago, and my weight hasn't varied more than a couple of pounds ever since.

Does this mean that all a person has to do is write down his goal and automatically he achieves it without doing anything further about it? Of course not. The point is that writing down the goal somehow got across to my "inner mind" the thing I wanted to accomplish—had gotten my "inner mind" to accept it—and the old resistance to achieving it, the old idea that I felt too miserable when I dieted, was gone. It enabled me to do the things that were necessary to get my weight down—and keep it there—which is just what the doctor ordered.

How a junior executive got a fast lift through writing down his goals

He was a very junior insurance company executive making $7,500 a year—which simply was not enough for his needs. He felt he had gotten into a rut. He was a bright young man, 32 years old, had a lovely wife and three fine children, owned a small home out on Long Island, and was head of a small department in an insurance company. He wanted his life to open up. He felt he was stagnating. He wanted a more vital existence.

I told him to write down his goals—which he did. As soon as he got at the typewriter his goals rolled out of him —and they were not small goals. They included: to become an officer in the company he now works for—to make $30,000 a year—to have a fine home in Westchester County —to take his wife on a European trip to visit her father, who is now living abroad—to provide for the education of his three children.

And this is the bombshell. As soon as he got his goals on paper there was an electric change in him. Seeing his goals written there before him gave him a new attitude right off the bat. To quote his own words, "I found my whole being suffused with an excited enthusiasm for my everyday business and surroundings."

He explained to me that before he had gotten his goals on paper he hadn't even thought of them as being goals but had always looked on them as just "some thoughts in my mind." Once he got these thoughts on paper they were magically transformed into goals—and once he saw them as his goals they flooded every minute of his life with meaning. He's now out of his rut and on the high road to the realization of his goals.

This technique works miracles—even for those who don't know what they want

You don't have to be able to come up with a list of bright, shining goals in order to get the enormous benefit of this technique. If you can make up a list of your goals right off the bat (the way the young insurance executive was able to), then all you have to do to set them on fire is to get them on paper.

But what if you don't know what you want? Can this technique of writing down goals help even then? It can.

I suggested to an older man—a man who had achieved impressive things in the past—that he get down on paper the things that he wants. He answered with some bitterness, "But I don't know what I want."

This is not unusual. Many people feel that they don't know what they want. Yet they're conscious of wanting something—and wanting it badly—and they're miserable. They have failed to find an outlet for their energies in the pursuit of some constructive goal—but they have to get rid of their energies—and they use them up in feelings of frustration, in resentment, boredom, worry. You can use up an awful lot of energy keeping up that kind of unhappiness.

But here again, the technique of trying to get some kind of goal on paper can come to the rescue even though you think you don't know what you want when you start. Montaigne used to say, "My appetite comes with eating," and in this case we can say that my goals come to me as I try to write them down. That's how it worked with the man I mentioned above. He told me a few days later that using this technique had enabled him to formulate a goal— that a vague idea which had been flitting around in the back of his mind had emerged as a goal—and he was greatly excited about it.

How the hottest companies in America are now using this technique of writing down goals

The corporate world has discovered the magic power of writing down goals. It has now become standard procedure in wide-awake companies for every department head to supply the president with a report of his aims for the year ahead—for the next five years—and for the next ten years. On the face of it this may seem silly—to expect anyone to be able to project his goals so far into the future. But corporations are the most pragmatic organizations in the world. They use this technique because it works.

One of the most enterprising companies in America— the leader in its field—requires all 50 of its vice presidents to write down their specific goals—short-range, medium-range, and long-range. It keeps things stirred up, gets everyone thinking ahead. It spurs the imagination to picture an effective future. It plants the "image seed" of things to come. It's made the company explosively successful.

How to insure fast progress on the goals you write down

As soon as you get any goal on paper, figure out something you can do at once toward its realization. You'll speed up your progress enormously by breaking down larger goals into short-range objectives on which you can take immediate action.

Example: a girl who was a typist in a large corporation wrote down the following as her main goal—

> I want to become secretary to the head of the company and to become so good at the job that I become indispensable to him—and I want to earn $10,000 a year.

Her present job was modest enough—typing from Dictaphone belts the memos the various executives of the company dictated to each other. As soon as she got her goal on paper she had the good sense to ask herself, "What do I do now?" As is usually the case, seeing her goal down in black and white before her set her imagination ablaze—and ideas for immediate action to quicken her goal came thick and fast.

She decided: (1) to begin reading attentively the memos she was typing (she reasoned rightly that these would give her a good grasp of what was going on in the company—would give her a background for her work as secretary to the top man); (2) she would send away at once for *The Complete Secretary's Handbook*—a book that she had heard was loaded with valuable information for anyone who was going to become a secretary, and which she had seen on the desks of several top secretaries in the company; (3) she knew that in order to become secretary to the top man she would have to become secretary to one of the lesser big men first—and she mapped out her strategy for getting such a job.

This method of first writing down your goal—and then writing down some immediate steps (no matter how small) you can take at once toward its realization—is the key to getting the things you want. It's your first great step for a great new life.

Why writing down your goals works miracles

The blazing success of this technique is in its ability to put across to your inner mind the goals that you want it to go to work on. The act of writing down your goals is the act that "sells" your goals to your inner mind. Once your inner mind is sold on your goals the battle is half won. You have gained a new and powerful ally. It immediately marshals all the resources of your being to achieve your goals. It works day and night to get you the things you have convinced it that you want.

Remember that this part of your mind which we call here the "inner mind" has no critical judgment of its own. It will accept any premise that you give it—and without question. It will work to get you anything—to fulfill any goal you are able to put across to it. But you must show it that you mean business—and writing down your goals is your first step to show it that you aren't just kidding about the things you say you want.

Once the inner mind is convinced, the big change takes place. Your goals are no longer obstacles to be overcome but are transformed as if by magic into throbbing sources of power. The goals become powerful generators—supplying the energy, the hope, the enthusiasm for their fulfillment.

Here is the mechanism that opens the floodgates of life. Here is the power to get you everything in life you want. Here is the answer to becoming strong—to living the victorious life—a life that will fulfill your heart's desires.

On the next page begins the exciting
Goal-A-Graph section—with the
ingenious forms that make it
simple to get your goals
on paper—and set
them on fire.

This specimen form—as filled in by Harold Masterson—is meant to give you the general idea of how the Goal-A-Graph is used.

The Goal-A-Graph
of
Harold Masterson

(Harold is 35 years old. He runs a department of 12 white collar workers. He earns $8,000 a year. The following are his job goals.)

1. **The spot I want:**
   I want to be head of a division of the company (including my own present department and three related departments —60 people in all). The division is now making half a million a year in profits. I want it—under my guidance—to make $2,000,000 a year.

2. **The income I want:**
   I want to make $35,000 a year as the highly successful head of this division—which should rate me (when I show $2,-000,000 in profit) a senior vice-presidency of the company.

3. **The personal capacity I want to develop:**
   I want to develop in myself a powerful combination of creative imagination and hard realism. I'm strong on imagination but need to balance it with hard practicality.

4. **My big pipe dream:**
   I want some day to own a substantial share of the company —to be a part of the real management—one of the boys who decides what happens.

Remember, the big thing is to fill out your Goal-A-Graph—to get a statement of your goals on paper—no matter how sketchy they may seem at first.

On the next page are the immediate actions Harold mapped out for doing something without delay toward the realization of the four goals written down above.

This is the second form—The Immediate Action Program—as filled in by Harold Masterson—the steps he planned to take at once—just to get himself started without delay on the aims written down in his Goal-A-Graph.

The Immediate Action Program
of
Harold Masterson

Immediate Action 1

Get up a list of ideas for making my present department more profitable.

Immediate Action 2

Start using the special ability I have to get people excited—get my department excited about making it the best in the company—hold a meeting and tell them the big things the department is going to do.

Immediate Action 3

Ask myself each day when I finish my work, "Have I achieved a good combination of creative imagination and hard realistic judgment?"

Immediate Action 4

Buy myself ten shares of the company's stock and get started on my pipe dream of someday owning a substantial portion of it.

Immediate Action 5

Before I go to bed each night review my Goal-A-Graph—paint mental images of how wonderful it will be to arrive at my goal.

Immediate Action 6

Start at once to give everything to my current job—to go all out on whatever the day brings.

Now you're ready for the exciting experience of filling in your own Goal-A-Graph and your own Immediate Action Program—the action that sets your goals on fire.

Five Important Hints for
Filling in Your Goal-A-Graph

1. This may be the most important moment of your life. The short time it takes to fill in your Goal-A-Graph can be the great turning point in your existence.

2. Even if you don't know what you want—don't let that keep you from filling it in. Do what you can with it. Your goals will tend to come to you as you try to write them down.

3. Work on your Goal-A-Graph after you have put in a good day's work in your current set-up (no matter how unsatisfactory it is). This will free you of the roadblocks that exist as long as you're fighting your current set-up.

4. Write up your goals in glowing terms—in language that will sell them to yourself—that will get you and keep you sold.

5. Give this a real go. The effort you invest in it can be repaid to you 10,000 times over. Be the one person in a hundred who's wise enough to take this electrifying action.

Now—to your personal Goal-A-Graph.

This form is for your own personal use.

The Goal-A-Graph of

_____

(your name here)

(Five spaces are provided below for writing down your special goals. Use as many of them as you need. Write down any goal you'd like to achieve, no matter how great it may seem. Remember this action has explosive power. When you write down your goals you bring into play the hottest psychological mechanism the human mind can use.)

Here are my goals:

1. ....
   ....

2. ....
   ....

3. ....
   ....

4. ....
   ....

5. ....
   ....

When you have finished filling in the above Goal-A-Graph—turn to the Immediate Action Form on the next page—and write down some step you can take at once toward each of your goals.

This form is for your own personal use.

The Immediate Action Program
of

_____

(your name here)

It's psychologically very important that you figure out some step you can take at once toward each goal written down on your Goal-A-Graph. These don't have to be big steps—but you should do something now—no matter how small—on each of them.

Immediate Action 1 ....
....

Immediate Action 2 ....
....

Immediate Action 3 ....
....

Immediate Action 4 ....
....

Immediate Action 5 ....
....

You don't have to use all five spaces above—use only those you need. It is not necessary to match the above Immediate Actions by number with the goals on your Goal-A-Graph. You may have written down just one goal on your Goal-A-Graph and may want to fill in three Immediate Actions above for that one goal.

*The next page gives you the exciting secret
of keeping your goals red hot.*

"Incendiary" follow-up keeps your goals blazing

Once you have (1) gotten your goals down on paper and (2) figured out some step you can take at once toward their fulfillment, you can vastly speed up your progress by (3) fanning the flames with this simple two-minute follow-up.

Here's the follow-up

Take two minutes each day to read over the goals you have written down. As you read them over you flash on the "screen of your mind" a picture of your goal fulfilled. This two-minute follow-up is dynamite. It keeps a fresh impression of your goal before your mind—and the big thing we're after here is to use the mind's enormous power to realize any picture that's kept before it.

All you need do is picture your goal. Don't worry about the ways and means necessary to reach your goal. You'll take care of that in the natural course of things if you keep before you the picture of what you want.

For example: A woman always wanted to own a real colonial home. She wrote down a statement of her goal: "I want to buy an authentic old colonial farmhouse—which I can turn into a charming, comfortable home—create a regular colonial gem." As soon as she (1) got her goal on paper, she (2) took her first immediate step (sent away to a real estate outfit for a catalog of farms for sale), and then (3) she used this two-minute follow-up to fan the flames of her burning goal.

Each day she read over her goal and flashed a picture of it on the screen of her mind. She had little money to work with, but she kept before her each day a blazing fresh impression of the thing she wanted. This enlisted every facet of her being in the pursuit of her goal. Her mind poured forth a continuous stream of ingenious ideas for its realization—ways to save money for it—ways to earn money for it—ways to track down bargain farmhouses that were for sale. She clipped out ideas from good magazines on colonial living. She grasped every opportunity to learn more about colonial furniture—colonial glassware—colonial decorating. Her mind became a powerful magnet that singled out from everything within reach anything that could further her goal—and when circumstances placed nothing in reach, she—like Napoleon—took the initiative and "created circumstances."

This technique for keeping your goal blazing before your mind works—and works fast. She soon found her farmhouse—a 1760 colonial. She was able to pick it up at a bargain price because it needed a lot of work—but it was solid and sound. She went to work on it—keeping her goal steadily before her. Today this authentic colonial farmhouse is one of the finest in New York State.

She realized her goal because she followed a sure-fire, three-step formula: (1) She wrote it down; (2) she took a step toward her goal just as soon as she got it on paper (sent for a real estate farm catalog); (3) each day she reviewed her goal to keep its image fresh and hot before her.

But I don't want a colonial farmhouse—I want a top executive job at $40,000 a year

It doesn't matter what you want, the formula is the same: (1) First write down your goal—get it on paper—"I want to become a top executive at $40,000 a year," and then (2) figure out something you can do at once toward its fulfillment (You might, for example, send off at once your subscription to *The Wall Street Journal*.), and then (3) each day read over your goal—spend two minutes flashing it on the screen of your mind, visualizing yourself in the top executive spot.

That's your sure-fire, three-step formula for setting and keeping your goals on fire. Remember, the more you keep your goal before your mind the hotter it becomes, the greater power it will generate for its own fulfillment.

This follow-up technique is so important that we have added this simple chart to make sure you use this technique for the next ten days while you're getting started.

Ten-Day Get Started Chart
For Keeping Your Goals Red Hot

The Chart below is for checking yourself on the daily use of the "follow-up" technique.

Check "Yes"—if you spent two minutes reviewing and vizualizing your goals.

Check "No" —if you neglected to do it.

1st day		2nd day		3rd day		4th day		5th day	
Yes	No	Yes	No	Yes	No	Yes	No	Yes	No

6th day		7th day		8th day		9th day		10th day	
Yes	No	Yes	No	Yes	No	Yes	No	Yes	No

On the next page is given
a 30-second recapitulation of this
terrific three-step formula for setting
your goals on fire and keeping them blazing.

Rapid Re-Cap of First Action

Here's the explosive three-step formula for setting your goals on fire and keeping them blazing.

Step One

Get a statement of your goals on paper. (Use the Goal-A-Graph supplied on page 32 for this purpose.)

Step Two

Figure out some immediate steps you can take toward your goals and take them. (Use the Immediate Action Program on page 33 for this purpose.)

Step Three

Review your goals and visualize them for two minutes each day. (Check your doing of this on page 36.)

Now get ready for Part II of this powerful book—in which we present three sizzling new actions—each of them a "switch-throwing" technique for releasing rock-like self-confidence.

HOW TO GAIN
TERRIFIC SELF-RELIANCE

This second section of the book is a regular power-house. It reveals three separate actions that flood one's whole being with electrifying confidence, rock-like self-belief.

Consider the power in these three actions—

Action I

This action demonstrates immediately to the self that it can rely on the self to do what it wants it to do. It sends a surging new reliance coursing through one's being the moment that it's tried.

Action 2

This little, almost mechanical action gets results out of all proportion to its size. It makes you terrific in all your contacts with others—gives you enormous assurance in dealing with anyone. Use it at once to multiply your personal influence in all your relationships.

Action 3

Here's a blockbuster—an action that spots your strongest talents and lets you go to town on them—that gives you the confidence that comes only with the feeling of talents in action.

Self-confidence in a very real sense is the whole story of achievement and the road to the enjoyment of life. These three actions trigger off con-fidence—fill the self with irresistible self-belief.

To give you
tremendous trust in yourself

This action is the fastest confidence-builder you can use. It goes right to the heart of this whole business of self-confidence—touches off a psychological landslide that releases self-reliance on a tremendous scale.

Here's the technique:

1. Make a special promise to yourself.
2. Write down the promise.
3. Carry it out for ten days.

For example: "For the next ten days I'm going to smoke 15 cigarettes a day instead of 30."

It doesn't matter too much what the promise is—but you've got to write it down—and come hell or high water you've got to keep it. When you make such a promise to yourself and keep it, you demonstrate to yourself that you can rely on yourself to do what you say you are going to do. This knowledge that you can rely on yourself is the basis of self-reliance.

Many people feel soft and weak inside. The reason for this feeling of weakness is too easy to see. It's simply this: these people know from experience that they can't count on themselves to see things through—they know that when the chips are down they will choose the easy way out—will choose the path that offers some momentary pleasure or ease instead of the harder path that gives them the greater over-all, long-range benefit. Why in heaven's name should they feel any reliance on the self when they know from a thousand experiences with the self that the self is not reliable?

This promise-technique—even when you use it in little things—changes everything fast—brings a new surge of self-reliance—proves to the self that it can count on the self—and that is the heart of the matter.

The man who didn't want any more wisdom

A brilliant and talented middle-aged man is very unhappy—and he's been unhappy for years. One evening when he was visiting at his friend's home the talk got around to books. His friend was telling him excitedly about a book he had just read:

"There's a lot of wisdom in that book. I found it very helpful. Would you like to take it along?"

The unhappy man's answer was a classic—

"No thanks, I don't need any more wisdom. I already

have more wisdom than I can use. What I need is the strength to apply some of the wisdom I already have. For example, I already know that I should work harder and be more careful with money. But I do neither."

His unhappiness stemmed from the fact that he knew he couldn't trust himself—that he never was willing to sacrifice some momentary pleasure for a longer range greater good. He knew himself well enough to know that he would never see anything difficult through to a finish. What was the use of his planning anything, or his thinking about things, or coming to any decisions? The whole business was pointless—nothing but shadowboxing—because his instrument of action, the operating self, the part of the self that carries out decisions with action simply wasn't working. It couldn't be relied upon, and he knew it.

There's enormous confidence-building power in keeping promises—whether to another person or to one's self. But for the purposes of using this technique we will deal in making promises to yourself. Here we control the whole process—we can set up any promise we like—and use it to get fast results.

Three cups of coffee with lunch

You may think we're becoming trivial when we talk about how many cups of coffee a person should drink. Frankly, we don't know how much coffee any person should have. Maybe you should drink a dozen cups of coffee a day and maybe you should drink Sanka. This little story concerns a young man who was drinking too much coffee. He'd have three or four cups every day with his noontime meal. It stimulated him enormously for an hour

or so, and he'd use this stimulation in brilliant lunch table
conversation. When the stimulation wore off, he could
hardly marshal his thinking processes at all. He felt spent,
nervously depleted—and wasn't good for much for the rest
of the afternoon.

He knew that this was no good for him—as surely as
anyone can know anything—but he kept right on with it. I
asked him why he didn't cut it down to one cup as long
as he had found out he felt so much better when he drank
only one cup.

"Because I don't have any guts, I guess," he answered.
"I've never had much will power. I guess I'm a weak person," and then he added as an afterthought, "I have little
self-confidence either, for that matter."

I could tell by the way he separated will power and
self-confidence that he didn't see the connection between
the two. He had without realizing it given me a perfect
opening to get right at the heart of this whole business of
self-reliance.

"Self-reliance comes when you find you have the will
power," I said, "when you find, you can rely on yourself to
carry out in your own life the wisdom experience points
out to you. Experience shows you every afternoon that four
cups of coffee are no good for you—that you should drink
one—and you go right on drinking four. How the devil can
you have any confidence in yourself when you can't rely
on yourself to profit from this very simple lesson?"

He laughed. "So all I have to do is to cut down to one
cup of coffee and I immediately become self-confident. I
become a man of iron."

"No, that's not quite the whole story. But it could be
your first step and a big one. Self-reliance comes when you

learn that you can count on yourself *not* to take the easiest path but the path of greatest profit to the self. When a man is sure that he can do this—then he knows he has himself in hand."

"I've never thought of it in that way. I'll consider it."

"No, don't consider it. There's no more considering to be done. You've had this lesson driven home to you for years. Write down a promise to yourself: 'For the next ten days I'll have one cup of coffee with lunch—and no matter what happens—stick to it.'"

I met him in the washroom one day a couple of weeks later. He told me, "You know, Bill, that technique works— and how it works! Every time I said no to another cup of coffee I could definitely feel an inner strengthening. There was something almost physical about it. It was as though the force within the temptation gave up when I resisted it and changed sides. It came over to my side and added its strength to my own."

"Congratulations. Are you going to keep up with the technique?"

"I sure am. I'm now looking around for new worlds to conquer—something else to build moral muscle out of."

The big shot industrialist who used this technique

Some years ago I used to visit the home of a big New York industrialist. He was rich, influential, had a terrific mind—but the biggest thing about him was his steely inner strength. It made him one man in a million. His rock-like self-assurance filled people with awe. He was so strong that I assumed he must have been born that way, that his enormous strength of character was a gift from nature. I

certainly never thought of him as ever using any technique
to develop confidence in himself.

But it was from this man that I first learned about using
this terrific technique. He told me he used it all the time—
ever since he first read about it in the writings of the great
psychologist, William James. It was this technique that
built his moral muscle and kept him so tough-fibred.

Always make a promise for a specific length of time

In telling me about the wonders this technique had
performed for him, he emphasized one point that made it
even more effective with him. He stressed the importance
of making every promise *for a specific period of time*. If
you're going to cut out smoking, don't just promise yourself
to cut out smoking—but promise yourself to cut it out for,
say, ten days.

He once promised himself to lay off cigars for a week.
He enjoyed smoking cigars. He felt they calmed his nerves,
enabled him to think more clearly—but he thought he
might feel better without them—and he wanted to experiment to find out. By the third day of his experiment he
had come to the conclusion that he was better off with
cigars than without them. But he would not let himself
smoke again till the week was up. He explained that there
were two reasons for this—

> *First*, a man can't let himself down—he can't treat
> lightly any promise he makes to himself—and
> *Second*, if you set a definite time limit you're
> more apt to stick it out for that limit.

When you set no time limit the pleasure-loving inner
self gets very cute in finding arguments to rationalize

getting its own way—but when you have your eye on, say, a ten-day pull, you're more apt to see it through—and by the end of the ten-day period you may have triumphed for good in whatever your promise was trying to achieve.

A man who can keep a promise is never bankrupt

In the gloomy depression years of the early 1930's a former big shot was having a particularly bad time. He had been a successful stockbroker and had made a lot of money. Now a few years later he was out of a job—his money was about gone and he wasn't getting any younger. Things looked pretty hopeless and he had begun to drink more than he should.

I know there is nothing unusual in that story. It was repeated in one form or another a million times over in the depression years. But this fellow had something that held him together—and it had to do with this technique.

One day his wife told him that her sister from the Middle West was coming to visit with them for a week in their small New York apartment. The sister was well-heeled, a teetotaller, very conservative, a bit strait-laced. His wife asked him to promise her that he would not take a drink of any kind for the week that her sister stayed with them.

He said O.K. he'd go along, he'd go on the wagon while her sister stayed with them.

His pal (drinking companion) called at the apartment one day while the wife and the sister were out. He had brought a bottle with him—and suggested that they have a drink.

"Sorry, Arthur, I can't. Alice's sister is spending a week

with us—and I promised Alice that I wouldn't drink anything while her sister is with us."

"Where are they now?"

"They've gone off shopping for the afternoon. Then
they're having dinner uptown—won't be back till late this
evening."

Arthur was thirsty and he didn't want to drink alone.

"But wasn't the reason your wife asked you not to drink
while her sister was here simply this: that she didn't want
her sister to see you drinking? Do you think she would
mean for you not to take a drink now—under these circumstances?"

"I don't know what she thought or what she would
expect me to do—but I do know what I promised. I told
her that I wouldn't take a drink all week."

"And you're going to keep that promise?"

"Yes, that's about all I have left—the ability to keep a
promise—and I'm going to hang on to it if I can. If that
goes then I'm done for."

This man made a strong comeback. He had a core of
iron left in him. He could keep a promise to himself—and
he could keep a promise to others.

What kind of promise should you make?

You can promise yourself anything. The big thing, of
course, is to start using this technique—to begin to gain
the enormous confidence-building power it provides. Just
promising yourself that you're going to do something—no
matter how arbitrary or silly it sounds—will work its fibre-
building magic for you. You could, for example, set your
alarm clock for two in the morning and when it goes off

make yourself get up and do a half hour's calisthenics. This would build moral muscle—but it would also be a bit looney.

It's sounder to try to kill two birds with one stone—to promise yourself something that you have found from experience is loaded with good for you. One of the most fruitful fields for this is the dreary-sounding area of "health habits." Then you get not only the confidence-building effect that comes from making a promise to yourself and keeping it—but you get the additional practical benefits that come from the action itself. For example, a man may have found that when he walks home from work at the end of the day (a half hour's walk) he feels so much better it changes everything. He's then glad to get home, enjoys his dinner more, enjoys the whole evening more, feels better all around—but he doesn't do this because the company bus is waiting there and he doesn't want to make the effort. Let him promise himself that for ten days he'll walk home from work—write down the promise and keep it. He gains on two counts—an immediate surge of self-reliance, plus all the physical benefits as well.

Don't fool around with this technique—It's loaded

This technique is a bombshell. Its benefits are enormous—but don't trifle with it. The dynamic psychological mechanism involved in this business works both ways. Keep your promise and it builds confidence fast—break your promise and it makes you less confident than ever. So promise yourself something that you can reasonably expect yourself to carry out. If you're smoking 30 cigarettes a day and you think you should smoke ten—but you don't think you'd be able to stick to ten—then promise yourself to smoke 15, for a starter, and when you have achieved that goal, pick your next goal and see that you make good on that.

I've seen this technique work wonders for people—rapidly develop within them a vein of iron—give them a self-reliance they've never known before—just by promising themselves something, writing down the promise—and keeping it.

Sample promises a person can make

Here are some specific examples of promises. (You will, of course, think up those that will have special meaning in your own life.)

1. *To keep my desk neat and orderly*
(One talented businessman thought he was such a genius that he was above keeping things in order—but, genius or not, he could never find anything on his desk. This simple promise immediately beefed up his production, increased his grip on himself.)

2. *To cut out the small talk*
(People of stature don't indulge in a lot of small talk. This area of "tongue control" is one of the fastest confidence-builders you can use. Try something here for ten days and feel the strength gather within you.)

3. *To limit yourself to one drink*
(This man used to have three drinks before dinner each night—felt incomparably better with one.)

4. *To help with the dishes*
(This young man and his wife both went to work. He

always listened to the news while his wife did the dishes. He promised to help with the dishes for ten days.)

5. *To cut out the continuous wisecracking*
(This girl was always being funny. This is the smart thing today—to sound like a TV comic. Here's a tremendous opportunity. Cut the wisecracks for ten days. It will set you aside from the chirping lightweights and every time you overcome the urge to say something funny your strength will go up along with your stock.)

6. *To limit one's self to an hour's television each evening*
(Nothing is more vitiating than a whole evening of indiscriminate television. For ten days limit yourself to one good program each evening.)

7. *Write down each day something new you've learned*
(This not only builds confidence—but it gives you a rich storehouse of precious material for continuous use.)

8. *Get up a half hour earlier*
(A friend of mine started each day with a disorganizing rush—gulped his breakfast—drove too fast to work—arrived ten minutes late. This promise was the opening wedge that changed his life.)

9. *Practice one hour a day at the piano*
(This housewife used to be a top pianist. She had lost a lot of her skill—decided to regain it.)

10. *Stop being the know-it-all at executive meetings*

(This man was bright—but at all executive meetings he played to the grandstand. He glibly supplied the answer to everything, was always horning in, telling everyone how to do things. He was a pain to everyone, disliked by the boss, resented by his peers, and inwardly displeased with himself.)

11. *Replace daydreams with action*

(This nice young lad indulged in too much daydreaming—picturing situations in which he glorified himself. He promised that each time he found himself daydreaming he would turn vigorously to the task at hand.)

12. *Whenever you feel like quitting—go on for an hour more*

(This man was ready to quit his work effort much too soon. He decided to make himself go on for an extra hour when he felt the usual urge to quit. This is difficult—but it pays off big.)

The way to the self-determined life

Promising yourself things like the dozen above—and keeping those promises—is the open road to the self-determined life. Thousands of people could dramatically change their whole lives with the magic of this discipline—with its vast confidence-building power.

We feel inadequate

The trouble with many of us is not that we lack brains, not that we lack education, not that we lack talent, not that we lack personality. Our trouble is that we feel that we will never be able to bring into being the kind of life we should like to lead.

This common feeling of inadequacy too often springs from the realization that we don't have ourselves in hand. When we feel that we can't count on our own selves, we then lack the self-reliance to choose our own course of action—to make the decisions that would realize ourselves.

The enormous paradox

When we lack this faith in ourselves, we still feel that we must place such faith in something. When a person can't have faith in himself he places it somewhere else. And the thing in which many such people place their faith —without ever realizing it—is *fear*. This is the greatest paradox—to place one's faith in fear—to count on fear to get one by. When you use fear as your method of operation, you can never act on your own. You can only react to events—and when you can only react, not act, you have lost the ability to lead a self-determining existence. You have lost the ability to take the action that will bring your individual talents into play.

This technique can start you off on a glorious self-determined existence

Here is the way to put the enormous power of this technique to work in your life. First, consider something that you're doing that you know from experience is not good for you—or something that you're not doing that you know from experience you should be doing. This is very much your own business. You know what it is. Choose it yourself.

Then, write down a promise to yourself—telling yourself that for the next ten days you'll carry it out in action. And no matter what happens see that you carry it out.

This will build self-reliance faster than anything else you can try. When you find that you have yourself in hand, everything will look different to you. You'll know for the first time what self-reliance means—because for the first time you'll know that you can rely on yourself.

For Putting the Technique in Action

1. On the next page is a list of hints for using this technique.

2. Then there are two "example pages"—showing how a man made a promise to himself and how it worked out.

3. Then there's a blank form for making your own promise to yourself and for checking your progress on it.

Hints for Using This Dynamic
Promise-Technique

1. Be sure to get in writing the promise you make to yourself—this gives substance to the whole idea. It's a *Must*.

2. Promise yourself something that calls for resolution—but don't make it so tough you won't have a chance.

3. Don't set up goals simply for the moral exercise (important as that is)—but try to kill two birds with one stone. Choose an action that gives you a "practical" benefit (other than strengthening your moral fibre).

4. Once you have promised yourself something—be sure to carry it out. (If you go back on your word it makes you still less confident.)

5. Remember that self-reliance comes with the belief that you can rely on yourself to carry out what you want to carry out.

6. Every promise should be for a specific period of time.

7. Don't be too quick to make promises. Remember that they're supposed to be carried out.

On the next page is a sample of one man's promise to himself—and why he made it.

Sample Promise

(Showing the promise a young executive made to himself.)

Background story

This young man lacked self-confidence. He didn't have himself in hand and he knew it. Because of his poor grip on himself he lacked the self-reliance that would have enabled him to bring to bear on his job his very considerable talents. **He lacked the self-discipline necessary for capitalizing on his abilities.**

He decided that his weakest point was this:

He would work brilliantly on his job for an hour or so and then he'd feel the urge to quit. After an hour's work he had had enough—wanted to fool around, indulge in small talk, call up somebody socially, read the newspaper.

Here is the promise
he made to himself.

Date *Jan. 1, 1964*

I promise myself that for the next *10* days I *will make myself go on for another hour's work whenever I have the usual urge to quit at the end of an hour's work.*

Signed *Arthur Johnston*

On the next page is a day-by-day record showing how the young man made out with his promise.

Here's the record of how the young man made out with his ten-day promise to go on for an hour when he wanted to quit.

	Kept It		**Remarks**
	Yes	**No**	
1st day	√		It was tough—but I did it.
2nd day	√		It seemed harder today than yesterday—but I didn't give up.
3rd day	√		I had just finished a one-hour stint and felt the usual urge to quit when George (the head of the department next to mine) dropped in. We usually chat for a while—but I excused myself and went on with my work.
4th day	√		Things went better today. I didn't have to fight so hard to go on for a second hour.
5th day	√		Told myself this whole thing is for the birds— that it's artificial and I ought to junk it—but kept my promise anyway (a little sullenly).
6th day	√		Getting used to the idea of working for longer periods. No trouble at all.
7th day	√		My assistant said to me today, "You seem to be awfully busy lately."
8th day	√		Getting a lot more work done—and was less tired at night than usual.
9th day	√		Worked steadily all day long. Things in my department are looking up.
10th day	√		I did it. Feel substantial inside. New ambitions are rising within me—and I feel confident about putting them over. This thing works!

On the next page is your own form for making a promise to yourself—and for keeping a ten-day record of how you make out.

YOUR OWN FORM (*for making your promise to yourself*).

Date............

I promise myself that for the next _____ days I will _____
_____
_____

Signed..................

How I made out with my promise:

Kept It

Yes   No   **Remarks**

1st day ....
....

2nd day ....
....

3rd day ....
....

4th day ....
....

5th day ....
....

6th day ....
....

7th day ....
....

8th day ....
....

9th day ....
....

10th day ....
....

Now you're ready for the next great
action—the magic "pad and points"
technique.

Action 2

To make you
terrific in all
your dealings with others

The purpose of this action is to give you tremendous new power in all your dealings with others.

Here's the technique:

Before you meet with anyone jot down on a pad
the points you want the contact to cover.

This sounds like just another one of those little helps a person should use. There's nothing little about it. The effect of this technique on others is electrifying. Its effect on yourself is pure magic.

For example: A schoolteacher was having a rough time with her principal. He was hounding her, finding fault with everything she did. She was a good teacher, doing a good job—but every week he'd call her down to his office and give her a good going over—and he always kicked about the same four or five things. For a long while she took it and said nothing.

Then I suggested to her that she use this "pad and points" technique. The next time the principal called her down to the office she was ready for him. She had written down five separate headings on a big pad—one for each of the areas in which he had criticized her work.

As soon as she came through the office door, the principal started his usual harangue. She told him, "Excuse me, but there are five questions I wish to ask you." She took the pad from under her arm and laid it before him on the desk. He couldn't have been more taken aback if she had belted him. He looked quickly at the pad, trying to find out what this was all about, and then looked up at her with a puzzled expression that had plenty of worry mixed in it.

The whole situation had changed at once. He was immediately on the defensive. He didn't like that pad with its five specific points. "What's this all about?" he wanted to know. He tried to sound forceful, but he had already started to run.

And she told him what it was all about:

"These are the five areas in which you have criticized my work—the five things you have found fault with at least ten times in the last few months. I want you to tell me now my specific weakness in each area that makes my work inadequate—and I want you to suggest what you would have me do in each area so I can give you what you want."

She picked up her pad, held her pen in readiness and said, "My first question is this . . ."

But he wouldn't have any part of it. He was now in full

flight. He tried to get out of the situation and still save his face (which was now pale with anger). He dismissed her with "You know very well what I want. See that you do it."

He never bothered her again.

I have seen a few points written down on a pad work their magic a hundred different times in a hundred different situations. There's a psychological element here that gives it a power out of all proportion to the action itself. Part of the magic comes from showing the other person that you're ready for him, part of the magic is the change in you because you have done your thinking first. But there's something that makes this "pad and points" technique a bombshell. The whole business has an over-all effect that's greater than the sum of its parts.

How the man with "pad and points" dominated a conference

A company president called a meeting of six department heads. (The company was considering bringing out a new product and the purpose of the meeting was to discuss the project.)

Arthur—the head of one of the departments involved— was a "pad and points" man. He spent the night before the meeting thinking about this new product problem, and the next morning when it was time for the meeting he was all set for it. He went to the conference with a big yellow pad on which he had written down nine points.

The other department heads had had a few thoughts on things, but they had written nothing down. They were going to do their thinking at the meeting. This is quite common in business today despite all the talk about business efficiency.

When the seven men were seated about the table the

president opened the meeting by announcing the topic and asked for their thoughts on it. After about 20 minutes of aimless discussion in which nobody but the president said anything much to the point, Arthur took his big yellow pad and placed it before him on the table.

He remarked modestly, "I have jotted down a few considerations we might want to discuss."

All eyes turned to Arthur and his pad with the nine points written on it. Arthur mentioned his first point, and it was discussed for 20 minutes. Then everyone looked to Arthur and his pad for the next point. Arthur dominated the meeting. For two hours it followed his outline. But Arthur had not only put his points on a pad. He was ready with carefully thought out observations on each of the points he had written down. He shone throughout the whole proceeding.

And he got a more tangible benefit. He wasn't interested only in looking good. He wanted this new product in his own department. As he went along he showed how his department was ready to handle the operation every step of the way. There was some kicking from other department heads when they saw what was happening—but they were no match for Arthur and his pad.

The president was so impressed with Arthur's performance, so sold on Arthur's ability to handle the new product that he gave the whole thing to his department. Result: $5,000,000 of high profit business for Arthur—which is not bad for an evening's work and a pad with nine points written on it.

The man who wouldn't make a phone call without it

This "pad and points" technique works its magic everywhere. I know one man who wouldn't make a phone call without jotting down the points he wants it to cover. It sums up in your own mind just what the phone call is to accomplish. It changes your whole manner when you make a call with your pad and points before you. You're well organized and you know it—and the other person senses your firm hold on things and responds with some efficiency of his own. And it saves the time and expense of calling back to cover some points you've forgotten.

The "pad and points" works wonders with your boss

There is no point where this technique pays off so fast and so big as when you want to see your boss about something. Most bosses, if they're any good, have too much to do. They're impatient with having the people who work for them come into their offices just to talk things over, fan the air, talk all around a problem.

Years ago I learned the value of a pad and points whenever I had to discuss anything with the boss. When I'd walk into his office I'd hold up my pad so he could see it—with each point numbered and circled—and say, "I have four things to go over with you when you have time." It always works its magic.

Any boss, no matter how busy he is, will try to give you a few minutes if he sees that you have done your own thinking first, that you have brought the problem up to the point where he must come in on it. But most employees go to their bosses for help without any recommendation of their own for him to consider, without any clean-cut questions for him to answer. They simply breeze in and announce a topic—"About that new collection letter—it's got to go out soon. I've been wondering what we ought to do about it."

The "pad and points" technique changes everything if you handle it right. It gives the boss something to get his teeth into. In effect you ask him to pass judgment on what *you* think should be done—and a good boss likes to operate that way. You get fast action from him—action that speeds up your effectiveness in your own job. It makes you stand out from the other employees. It makes you welcome in the boss's office any time you want to go in.

And the boss himself should use this technique

I've seen big bosses—the biggest of them—company presidents, big sales executives, make a mess of interviews and meetings all because they failed to use this "pad and points" technique. The ablest company president I ever knew used this for everything. Before he'd call in a vice president, even for a five-minute discussion, he'd first jot down the main points he wanted to go over with him and run through a mental rehearsal of what he wanted to say on each point. He did the same thing with great care before he called an executive meeting. The saving in time was terrific. He'd get more things done in a half-hour meeting than most business leaders would accomplish in an all-day conference. When you left him you felt good about things—you felt that something had been settled and everyone knew his role in carrying out the decisions that had been made.

One of America's selling giants calls it a miracle

One of the greatest salesmen in America uses this "pad and points" technique and attributes his king-sized income to it. He makes it part and parcel of every interview. The pad he uses is really a stenographer's shorthand notebook. At the top of the page he writes the prospect's name in large letters, and under it he lists the points he's going to make.

At the strategic moment he opens the notebook and lays it before the prospect. The prospect always shows interest in seeing his name written out at the top of the page—and when he sees the specific points listed he knows the salesman has prepared for the call, has something important to say, isn't going to waste his time.

The man has cleaned up with this technique. It forces him to be prepared. It enables him to mentally rehearse every interview before he has it. And the biggest factor of all is the psychological factor of producing the pad and points itself.

No place is too small for this technique

Some years ago a young advertising copywriter came to me and asked if I would give my opinion of a letter he had written. The usual procedure in this case is for the veteran to read it over, think about it for a few minutes and tell the tyro what he thinks. But even here I used the "pad and points" technique. It meant, to begin with, that I had to give some serious thought to his letter in order to come up with several specific points of criticism that were important enough to write down (the pad and points technique makes you do a better job with everything)—but the big thing was the way it impressed the young copywriter. It meant infinitely more to him than just rattling off a few comments.

After I had gone over with him the points I had written

down, I left with him the "pad and points" I had made up in criticism of his letter. The next time I went into his office I saw that he had taped the sheet to the wall next to his desk. He realized that I had bothered to do a good job in passing judgment on his work and he took it ten times as seriously as any oral comment I might have made.

This technique can change you in ten days

Use this "pad and points" technique for ten days. It immediately gives you a feeling of confidence—the sense of being armed for combat. It brings a dynamic new power, a new-found influence to all your contacts with others.

The Blueprint-for-Action section

The next few pages are most important of all—the business-end of the chapter. This "get-going" material will enable you to slide right into using this high-powered technique.

These "blueprint pages" give you

1. A rapid-fire summary of vital hints for using the technique.

2. A suggestion list of a dozen situations where it can be used.

3. A sample "pad and points" all filled in.

4. A handy form for you to use in trying out this little giant of an action.

Quick summary of hints is on the next page.

"Pad and Points" Technique in Action

Five hints for using "pad and points" technique:

(a) Keep a few pads handy. (I keep a small one on the telephone table at home—larger ones on my work desk and by my easy chair.)

(b) State at the top of the sheet what the main objective of the contact is, the goal for which you're using this technique. (This alone will sharpen your whole attack.)

(c) Think through the main points you want this contact to cover and write them down.

(d) Hold a quick mental rehearsal of each point before you meet your man.

(e) Follow what you have written down. (Just writing down the points will help you even though you don't refer to them—but be sure to refer to them.)

Here is a list of a dozen situations where the "pad and points" technique gives dynamic, incisive help:

1. When you must see your boss.
2. Buying anything (a house, a car, life insurance).
3. Seeing your child's teacher about his work.
4. Getting a loan at the bank.
5. Having someone do a job in your home.
6. Seeing your doctor.
7. Making a phone call.
8. Talking with an employee about his work.
9. Presiding at a meeting.
10. Selling something.
11. Getting your car serviced.
12. A talk with someone in your family.

The whole attitude of the person on the other side changes when you use "pad and points." You get attention, respect, co-operation.

Sample "Pad and Points"

(as made up by a minor boss in the shipping department
for interviewing his boss—a company vice president)

1. This contact is with .... *Mr. Barlow*
2. The objective of the interview .... *To get Mr. Barlow's O.K.*
on a new shipping carton that will reduce
breakage in transit.

Points to cover

(a) *Breakage is running 8% — shockingly high.*

(b) *The trouble is the carton — should use a new*
tough "honeycombed" carton.

(c) *Have tested new carton — banged it around, dropped*
it, thrown it against wall — but no breakage.

(d) *Carton costs two cents more each.*

(e) *Will save $800. a week net — and much more in re-*
lated expenses — to say nothing of good will.

(f) *Suggests we junk leftover cartons.*

(g) *Can get new cartons in ten days.*

(h) *Suggest we order 100,000*

(i) *Have tried new carton for 100 trial shipments — no.*
problems in handling, no returns for breakage.

(j) *Suggest Mr. Barlow O.K. immediate change over*
to new carton and that we order today.

Result *Mr. Barlow checked with our purchasing and*
accounting departments while I waited. They
confirmed my figures and judgement.
Mr. Barlow told me to go ahead.

"Pad and Points" Form (for your use)

Date..................

This contact is with.......................................

The objective of the interview.............................

....

....

Points to cover

(a) ....

(b) ....

(c) ....

(d) ....

(e) ....

(f) ....

(g) ....

(h) ....

(i) ....

(j) ....

Result ....

....

To bring
your hottest talents
dramatically into play

The purpose of this magic action is to uncover your talents, let you go to town on your richest gifts, give you the exhilarating self-confidence that comes with capacity in action.

Here's the technique:

Jot down on the form supplied at the end of this chapter any "show-through" of talent you've had in the past or any new "show-through" that comes along currently—and then give these talents the electric follow-up treatment.

In ten days this technique can break your life wide open.

Here's the exciting background story

Every person can do something at which he's a natural. But the manifestations of these big talents are often given to us in little things. The "show-through" seems unimportant. The little successes which hint at great capacity we think of no account—and we fail to take the vital "follow-up;" we fail to capitalize on our greatest gifts.

The most important thing that can happen to you is to find that there's something you can do easily and well. These "talent show-throughs" are dynamite. They're great flashing lights signaling enormous potential, showing where your real power lies.

A talent isn't something separate from you like the watch you wear on your wrist. Your talents are you. They suggest the make-up of your whole being. They point out the direction in which your capacities are virtually unlimited.

The path to victorious living is to watch for these talent "show-throughs"—to take decisive action upon them. As soon as you begin to use these powers that are you—you gain immediate self-confidence, multiply your success.

The young matron who wanted social success

This young matron wanted to play a more active role in the social life of her rather ritzy suburban community. She lacked self-confidence and had no idea how she could achieve what she was after.

Then she remembered something from her college days —that whenever she'd tell another person about a book she had read, the person would become excitedly interested in

what she had to say. Here was a "talent show-through"—
she had a talent for telling about the books she had read.
She could give a ten-minute review of a book that was not
only a good summary of its highlights—but an exciting
experience for the person who listened to it.

She had never done anything before to capitalize on
this little "show-through" of talent. She thought, "So
what?" as you probably do. But this is just the kind of thing
we're talking about. As soon as we explained to her the
magic of "talent show-through and follow-up" she saw in
this little talent the answer to her problem. She spoke to
the president of her social club—told her that she had just
read a book and would like to give a talk on it at the next
meeting.

The talk was a spectacular success—so good, in fact,
that the club asked her to make her talks on books a feature
of each meeting. They soon became the outstanding event
in these meetings—raised the tone of the whole organization.

Now what's the point of all this? It's this. As soon as
you go all out on some talent that experience has shown
you you have, your life gets off the ground with a roar,
everything turns to success—and a vast surge of confidence
comes rushing in as you feel the strength of your talents in
action.

In ten days you can start a revolution in your life if
you will make a list of your talent "show-throughs"—and
then use "follow-up" on them. (When you have finished
reading this chapter, use the forms that follow it in the
"Blueprint-for-Action" section. They make it simple for
you to use this explosive technique.)

You can use this dynamite no matter where you are— no matter what your job

Burt was a life insurance salesman—doing a mediocre job—making $7,000 a year. He was a prime example of how a man can lose out when he fails to exploit a "talent show-through."

Burt worked hard. He handled about a hundred interviews a month. About once a month he would call on some big shot, usually a company president. He was always a bit nervous about making these calls on business tycoons, but he had no more trouble getting in to see them than he had with smaller prospects and, surprisingly, his batting average per call was even better with these king-sized prospects than with the small fry.

The minute he got talking with a big man his nervousness disappeared. There was something about the way he talked with big people that they liked. He had an easy manner with them, free of the usual subservience that big men are used to—and so sick of. But despite his success with these men he saw so few of them that he was selling only two or three big policies a year to these high-caliber prospects.

Here was a "talent show-through" with a vengeance. The alarm bell was sounding; the signal light was flashing. But Burt never used "talent follow-up" to capitalize on it. Here he was with a special talent that could be turned into a gold mine—and he was sitting on it, doing nothing about it.

This went on for a couple of years till Burt got a new salesmanager. When the salesmanager found that Burt could talk with big people and sell them, he wanted to know why Burt hadn't capitalized on the enormous potential it indicated.

Burt told him that he always felt nervous when he went to call on a big man and he wouldn't want a steady diet of it. The salesmanager explained to him that his nervousness would disappear as soon as he went all out on the special talent he had for dealing with big people, that self-confidence is a question of feeling the strength of your talents in action.

A few years ago I heard Burt give a talk to a group of insurance men. He was one of the top men in the company —and it was one of the larger companies. He told his story. He said the thing that puzzled him was his slowness in recognizing the enormous potential of this "show-through" —that it took him so long to follow up and capitalize on it—this special talent for dealing with and selling big people.

As soon as he used this technique of "talent show-through and follow-up" his income shot into the upper brackets—and the salesmanager's prophecy was right. When he brought into play his special strength for dealing with high-caliber prospects, the pre-interview nervousness he used to feel disappeared. Using his real strengths gave him immediate confidence—as it always does. He told us that he could now sell almost every big man who would give him a hearing—and a great many of them did.

"Talent show-through and follow-up" enabled me to write a million-dollar letter

Some years ago I was writing advertising letters selling books by mail. I was selling business books to executives, accounting books to accountants, books on legal subjects to lawyers and books on salesmanship to salesmen. Whenever I wrote a letter to salesmen it hit the jackpot. My letters selling books to salesmen did better than anything else I wrote.

Here was a "talent show-through"—a narrow little thing to be sure—but it was emphatic. The bell was ringing; the light was flashing—but I did nothing to capitalize fully on it. Whenever it came time to write a letter on a selling book I wrote it—got good results with it—and did nothing more about it. I went along with things as usual for months. Then for no apparent reason (and months late) I got the idea that I should do something about this "show-through." I decided to figure out some way that would capitalize on it.

I suggested to my boss that we get out a really superior course for salesmen—not just another $5 book—but a humdinger that would sell for around $15 and be worth it. I knew from years of selling experience what salesmen needed—and I wrote up an outline of what should be in the Course. I wrote the best letter I knew how to write to sell the Course. We mailed it out and waited. As soon as results started coming in I knew that we had hit it. The whole project was fantastically successful. The first letter I wrote brought in over a million dollars worth of orders.

This technique of "talent show-through and follow-up" is dynamite—even in cases like this where the talent is off-beat and seemingly unimportant. But you must take the initiative with these little "talent show-throughs" and not let them lie there unused. A bit of ingenuity in creating ways to capitalize on them brings enormous results. Any person can do this. It brings exciting new success fast—and it sends a surge of self-belief coursing through you such as you've never known before.

Management gets into the act

Here again we can take a lesson from the hottest companies in America—watch what they're doing in this field of "talent show-through and follow-up." The smartest companies are exploding with profits because they are trying to use to the full the special talents their people have. They have realistically accepted the iron fact that people are what they are. They don't try to change them—they take them as they find them and try to turn their special abilities into profit. As soon as they find a man has a talent for any one thing they go all out on it—give him every opportunity to bring it into play—allow him to create opportunities for turning it into greater company success.

This works miracles at the company level—but it can work magic for you personally if you will bring this technique of "talent show-through and follow-up" vigorously into play on your own.

Do you remember the story of "Acres of Diamonds," in which a man wanders all over looking for riches—and comes back to find diamonds in his own back yard? We too look all over for opportunities for happiness, for satisfaction, for fulfillment—and all these things are much closer to us than our own back yards. Your talents are already in you, ready to go, waiting to be used. They don't need another thing. All you need to do is to watch for the flash of the "show-through" and then use your ingenuity and energy to exploit these talents to the full.

The young man who thought he wanted to be a banker

There's nothing but heartache and misery for people who won't listen to their true talents and give them a chance. Some of the sorriest examples of unhappiness in life are the tragedies of the unfulfilled. Here is a sad story with a happy ending.

This young man lived in a small town a couple of hours outside of New York City. His older brother had gone to live in the city some ten years before and his first job was with a big bank. By the time the older brother was 30 he was already a successful New York banker. The biggest story in this little town was the meteoric rise of the older brother to the top of the banking field. All the younger brother heard for years was talk of his brother's success. He came to believe that the only kind of success worth having was the kind his brother had made. When he graduated from college he did what everyone expected of him and what he expected of himself. He got a job with a New York City bank.

It was murder. He had no talent for banking and no interest in it. He studied books on banking till he was blue in the face. He was killing himself working on an ambition that had nothing to do with his talent or temperament. He was bright enough—had an IQ of 140—but it didn't seem to help. He read one book on foreign exchange three times but couldn't make the stuff stick in his head. A month later he would have been hard put to tell what foreign exchange was all about. In a couple of years he cracked up and came home feeling at 25 that his life was a failure—and all because he had tried to be something other than what his experience indicated he should be.

His old friend straightens him out

He had a good friend in this small town—a former high school buddy—a fellow of sense and understanding. This friend straightened him out. Here's what he told him:

"When I saw you go off to follow in your brother's footsteps I smelled trouble—but I said nothing. You seemed so set on becoming a banker. But your whole experience in high school suggested something other than banking. A fellow isn't one thing in school and a wholly different thing somewhere else. You had a feeling for words, you could write a good theme, give an excellent talk. You were loaded with ideas—and you knew how to dramatize them. You were no good at analytical thought, at forming tough-minded judgments. You chose the banking field because of your brother's success. You were foreordained to failure in it. Everything in your experience pointed to something other than banking as your field."

His friend continued with this common sense observation—

"I don't go along with the nonsense that a man can do only one thing and that he must get into the work that suits him to a T—but he should get into something that generally matches his talents and temperament. Your own successes suggested something like journalism, or advertising, or teaching." He went into advertising. As soon as he touched this field everything sprang to life. He was an immediate success. The very qualities that made him a flop as a banker now became assets in advertising.

Self-reliance means something more than belief in your ability to handle things

Self-reliance is not only the belief that you can handle things and become successful. It's something more than that. It includes having the courage to listen to your talents for a hint of the kind of success you should want. It means taking your cue from what you are—not listening to something outside yourself to get an idea of what you should become. When we follow the kind of life that our talents and our temperament tell us to follow we are happy and we are successful. We are ourselves and we are strong.

Stop crawling and start flying

You can break things wide open if you will start to use at once this technique of "talent show-through and talent follow-up." Watch for any sign of talent. Then give it the gun in action. Figure out ways you can bring it into play. Magnify your talent in your own mind—magnify it in action.

The Blueprint-for-Action section

The following pages are the business-end of this chapter. They have all been carefully worked out to make it simple for you to use this dynamic technique.

> *First*—There are half a dozen rapid-fire examples of how people have gone to town on their talents. These will whet your appetite.

> *Second*—There's a form on which to jot down the "talent show-throughs" you have had in the past—and a

form for jotting down new "show-throughs" as they come along.

Third—There's the all-important "follow-up" form (where you figure out the ways you're going to go to town on the big inner talents hinted at by your "show-throughs.")

Now turn to the next page and start using this success-making, confidence-building technique.

A special exercise to test your imagination and ingenuity in capitalizing on "talent show-throughs."

Six Talent "Show-Throughs"
of Six Different People

Here are six "little" talent "show-throughs." The possibilities they offered for "follow-up" might easily have been neglected. Try to imagine what could be done with each of them. Each of them was turned into a dramatic success.

1. *Bows and arrows:* A man's hobby was archery. He tried making his own bows and arrows. They turned out to be masterpieces.
   What follow-up can you suggest?

2. *Bread:* A woman baked a few loaves of old-fashioned whole-wheat bread for her family. The bread was so good everyone wanted it.
   What follow-up can you suggest?

3. *Speeches:* A young man with a small-time job had never made a speech in his life. When he was asked to give one it turned out to be terrific.
   What follow-up can you suggest?

4. *Teaching:* A young clerical worker discovered he had a special flair for teaching his fellow workers the tougher parts of their jobs—was able to make difficult things crystal-clear.
   What follow-up can you suggest?

5. *Discussion:* A middle-aged man found that whenever he discussed psychological and philosophical subjects with a social group in someone's living room, people were excitedly interested in what he had to say.
   What follow-up can you suggest?

6. *Headlines:* A retired businessman found that he had a talent for making up attention-getting advertising headlines.
   What follow-up can you suggest?

Anyone of these "show-throughs" could have been let alone—not capitalized on.

Turn to the next page to see how each one was given the "follow-up" and turned into electric success.

Here are the six exciting "follow-up" stories

1. *Bows and arrows:*

One day a number of years ago when I was taking one of my long hikes through the backwoods I came across an archer who was carrying a beautiful six-foot bow—one of the most handsome bows I had ever seen. I stopped to express my admiration for it. He was a friendly young man —told me that archery was his hobby and that he had made the bow himself. He took a few shots to show me how accurate the bow was—and I was flabbergasted by his rifle-like proficiency. To be able to make such a beautiful and effective bow (and arrows) was a red-hot "talent show-through." Before we parted we introduced ourselves to each other and went on our way.

A few years later I was in a fine New York shop and I saw a rack full of bows. This young man's name was on a number of them. I later found out that he had gone into the manufacture of archery equipment—that he was doing a thriving business—that his products were nationally known —that he himself had become a recognized authority on archery. A perfect example of "talent show-through and follow-up."

2. *Bread:*

When Mrs. Margaret Rudkin baked a batch of good old-fashioned whole-wheat bread for her family, it turned out to be so wonderful everybody wanted it. That's how Pepperidge Farm products got started in Connecticut some 25 years ago. Last winter when I was vacationing in southern Texas, I was pleased to see that Pepperidge Farm whole-wheat bread was available there—and was very pleased to buy it—and still more pleased to eat it.

The success of Mrs. Rudkin—and her wonderful products—has now become something of a legend. The enterprise now has plants in several states—now makes a whole line of super-delicious baked goods—all of them filled with honest-to-goodness old-fashioned quality. Here was a "talent show-through and follow-up" of heroic proportions. Mrs. Rudkin has not only become outstandingly successful —but she has done millions of us a great service.

3. *Speech:*

One day a big boss asked a young employee with a small-time job if he would give a talk to the executives in the company and explain the special work he was handling. The young man surprised himself and everyone else by giving a terrific talk. He held the big shots spellbound— made a series of hard-hitting, profit-making points that went off like a 21-gun salute.

When he told his wife about his "show-through" she urged him to get busy with some "follow-up" on it. He volunteered to give talks (*gratis*—and in the evening) to various men's organizations. One night the head of a large corporation was in the audience. As soon as he heard the young man he wanted him—he needed a profit-minded point-maker of such forcefulness in his own organization. The young man stepped from his little job into a good one —but perhaps even more important was the upsurge in confidence that came with bringing his talents into play.

4. *Teaching:*

This young man noticed time and time again his one "little" talent "show-through." He could teach—make things clear to others. When he would explain things to his fellow workers they'd get the point at once. Everyone was impressed. He often heard the comment, "For Heaven's sake, you should have been a teacher."

But he didn't want to be a teacher. He worked for a large insurance company and wanted to be successful in it. I told him to try to find some way to capitalize on his talent within his organization.

He asked for an interview with his big boss (the vice president in charge of his end of the organization). He told him about his "teaching ability"—how he could quickly make things clear to people when no one else was able to— asked if there were any place in the company where his strong point could be used to advantage.

He's now head of a division in the company—in charge of a lot of young people whose job it is to handle difficult policyholder problems. He's tops at giving these young folks the training and the insight that they need. He's a regular whiz at the job. He used "follow-up" on his "show-through" and went to town. He feels the strength of his talent in action—is confident, respected, successful.

5. *Discussion:*

A middle-aged man found that he immediately became the center of any "living-room group" the minute the talk got around to psychology and philosophy. People would hang on his words—ask him all kinds of questions. He seemed to be able to give them just what they wanted. He was not profound—but he could talk psychology and philosophy in a practical everyday-problem vein that hit people "right where they live."

He had never done anything with this talent—thought

of it as an off-beat something of no special account—but his "popularized treatment" of these subjects was so apt, so interesting that several of his friends urged him to write a popular book covering the same matters he so brilliantly discussed.

His book is about to be published. The editor says it's great. The advance demand for it is heavy.

6. *Headlines:*

A retired businessman discovered that he could make up much better advertising headlines than he saw in the magazines. He could sit down for an hour and knock off a dozen beauties.

Some of his friends were advertising men. They showed immediate interest in his headline creativity. He has now parlayed this "show-through" into a big "follow-up" payoff. He has made a good thing out of doing nothing but supplying different advertising outfits with lists of headline-advertising ideas.

The variety of these "show-throughs" is endless. Watch for yours. Anything you have a flair for suggests enormous opportunities. Use your ingenuity for finding a "follow-up" on which you can go to town. Use your talents. Turn them into confidence and success.

On the next page is an invaluable form to launch you out on this electric technique—for jotting down your own "talent show-throughs" that have come through in the past.

Special form for your use.

My Own "Talent Show-Throughs" in the Past

Write down here any activity you've shown a flair for—in school —in church work—in club work—in social life—in business— around the house—anything you've found you can do easily and well. Never mind how small or silly it sounds.

(Such "show-throughs" are just hints of the vast potential capacity locked up within you.)

1. ....
   ....

2. ....
   ....

3. ....
   ....

4. ....
   ....

5. ....
   ....

A few minutes spent reviewing your past for "show-throughs" of talent and jotting them down could prove the hottest investment of time you've ever made.

On the next page is the form for recording your new "talent show-throughs" as they come along.

Special form for your use.

My New Discoveries of "Talent Show-Throughs"

Keep an eye on yourself—watch for current "show-throughs" as they come along—and record them in the space below.

Date   **New "talent show-throughs"**

1. . . . .
                            . . . .

2. . . . .
                            . . . .

3. . . . .
                            . . . .

4. . . . .
                            . . . .

5. . . . .
                            . . . .

As soon as you spot anything that you have a flair for —don't let a minute go by without jotting it down. Keep the book handy. It's your "desk manual" for finding the victorious life.

Now—to the next page—the most vital part
of the whole technique—the special form for
the "follow-up."

Special form for your use.

My Vital Talent "Follow-Up"

Use your ingenuity to figure out some way you can go to town on the special talents hinted at by your "talent show-throughs" (as recorded on the two previous forms).

This is the vital part of the whole technique—what you do about the "show-throughs" you have jotted down on the two preceding pages.

My "talent show-through"   **Dynamic "follow-up" action**
(from either of two
preceding forms)

1. . . . .
                                          . . . .
                                          . . . .
2. . . . .
                                          . . . .
                                          . . . .
3. . . . .
                                          . . . .
                                          . . . .

Remember that the purpose of this technique is not merely to make you more successful (it will do that with a vengeance)—but to get you using the big talents that are locked up inside you, to let you feel the strength that comes with using them, to give you confidence such as you've never known before.

Now we're ready for PART III of this book's great liberating program—

"HOW TO UNLEASH YOUR FULL MENTAL POWERS"

PART III

HOW TO UNLEASH
YOUR FULL MENTAL POWERS

This third section of the book is terrific. It shows you how to throw the switch—release your full mental powers.

Here are the three electric actions—

Action 1

This action sets off the mind's unlimited capacity for creating ideas. The fastest way to wake things up, to get over into victorious living is to tap this great idea-reservoir. This action ignites the process, gives you a continuous supply of hot ideas.

Action 2

This simple action supplies the mind with exciting new facts and insights to work with—ready every second to come to your aid. This power-packed information makes you a new individual—gives you vital forceful things to say, enables you to move with surging new power.

Action 3

This action immediately steps up your judgment—makes you a decision-maker. It gives you the psychological key to all judgment—the key to effective thinking.

Most people don't begin to use their mental powers—but these three actions will rip their powers wide open—enable them to live in a brighter, happier, more successful world.

*Let's go to the next page and see how to get
some exciting new ideas.*

To release
the mind's enormous potential
for getting ideas

The purpose of this action is to prime the pump—to tap the enormous potential of the inner mind for coming up with ideas.

Here's the technique:

Put a sheet of paper in your typewriter (or pick up a pad and pencil) and jot down all the ideas you can think of on a given subject.

This simple action primes the pump of the inner mind and can give a person more good ideas in a week than most people come up with in a year. It's dynamite for anyone who has a problem—whether it's a woman whose problem is to find herself a job—or a tycoon who wants to double the size of his corporate empire.

Your unlimited idea potential

The potential of the human mind for creating new ideas is unlimited. Everyone has a storehouse of thousands and thousands of facts and impressions in his memory—and these facts and impressions can be combined in an endless variety of ways to create an endless number of ideas.

When your mind comes up with an idea it has taken two or more separate facts that were lying unconnected in your memory and flashed their relationship.

Example: The following four pieces of information were lying separate and unconnected in a man's mind:

1. A week ago he learned that the 100-acre Butler farm five miles out of town is for sale.

2. Six months ago he saw an obscure notice in the local paper that the township was going to surface the back-country dirt roads.

3. He knows that a large corporation is going to build a new plant in town and will hire 3,000 new employees.

4. He recently went with his son looking for a home for him and his family and found an acute housing shortage in the town.

It's easy enough to see the relationship of these four facts now that we've run them off together. They suggest a money-making real estate opportunity such as the following:

> You can buy the farm—which will now be easily accessible over the improved roads—and sell it as a real estate development—to house the new employees at the new plant in town.

But in order for the mind to "flash this relationship" and come up with the idea, it had to choose these four facts from among thousands of impressions stored in its memory. For a genius, this business of flashing relationships of unconnected facts into creative ideas is a spontaneous process—and if you're a genius you won't need this chapter —but there are only a couple of such geniuses in a generation.

The rest of us need some kind of discipline that will stir the unconscious mind into this creative process. If you're like most intelligent people, your mind, left to its own devices will come up with 3 or 4 good ideas a year— but with this technique you touch off this "flashing mechanism," come up with 30 or 40 ideas and really set your life on fire.

The simple technique that primes the pump

For the next few days take ten minutes a day to jot down lists of ideas. Make yourself do it. Force yourself to write down a list of six or eight ideas on any subject you like. You can make up a list of exciting new ideas for increasing your income, or a list of new products for your company to bring out. You can jot down ideas for saving money in your household, ideas for getting a better job, or doing a better job in your present work, or a list of ideas for opening up your social life, or for keeping your wife (or your husband) happy.

Don't worry about how good the ideas you write down may be at the start. The purpose of making up these lists is to prime the pump of the subconscious mind, to trigger off its vast potential creativity, to start it flashing relationships. Don't feel let down if the first list you come up with has nothing usable in it. The main thing is to come up with your pump-priming list.

A department head makes up a list

Here is a list of ideas made up by the head of a white collar department of "semi-creative" people. His people weren't turning out enough work. He jotted down the following possibilities:

1. Check with everyone at 4 o'clock to see how his work is coming.
2. Ask each person in the department to write down what he plans to accomplish in the coming week.
3. Put up a chart showing the job units each person completes each month.
4. Insist that people get down to work at starting time.
5. Get one suggestion from each person in the depart- ment on what he thinks would speed up the work.
6. Set deadlines when jobs should be finished.

Six ideas were all he could think of in his first ten- minute session, and when he looked his list over he thought pretty poorly of the lot. But when he looked them over again a few days later, he rather liked Number 6, "Set deadlines when jobs should be finished." It kept coming back to him again and again.

The people in his department did a kind of work where no deadline is called for. When they finished up a job it was put through the hopper. Because they did work that was "creative" they thought they had the right to take their own time—to work when the spirit moved them, which of course is horse feathers.

He decided to set deadlines on every job. He had to think up a way to justify the deadlines and he told his people that the work was now going to be integrated with schedules in other departments (which was partly true).

The deadline idea worked miracles—and right from the start. People stopped toying with their work and began to get things done. He made his deadline idea still more effective by backing it up with another idea from his list (to check at 4 o'clock each day to see how each person was coming along). These two steps doubled production in his department—and this whole change came from the simple technique of making up a list of ideas.

These lists are terrific time bombs

At times a list of ideas will have nothing usable in it, but this doesn't mean that the effort that's gone into the list is wasted. If you've sweated out your list and still not gotten the juicy idea you've been looking for, *then the hard work you've done on the list sets off a cerebration in depth —the work continues in the inner mind and the hot idea comes through later.*

This list technique often primes the pump immediately and gives you a good idea right off the bat—but when it doesn't, the "list work" serves to light the fuse and the idea comes through with explosive force later when you least expect it.

The list that yielded a jackpot idea three weeks later

An advertising man was given the job of coming up with an idea for selling a brand-new product the company was bringing out. He sat at his typewriter for an hour and sweated out 26 headline ideas for the ad. When he finished he looked the list over and told himself that it was just no good. He was an easily discouraged person, as advertising writers are apt to be, and he concluded that he had failed and asked the boss to give the assignment to someone else. The boss said they'd wait a while and see what happened.

Three weeks later when the ad man was spading his garden the time bomb went off. The idea he had been looking for hit him like a bolt from the blue. It was such a juicy idea it sent his career skyrocketing. It made money for the company hand over fist.

Where had this sockdolager of an idea come from? It had come from the "no good list" of ideas he had made up—the list that he thought was useless. When he looked back at his fruitless list he was easily able to trace the origin of the jackpot idea. If he had not made up that list he would never have gotten his winning idea. The hour's work of making up the list had lighted the fuse; the subconscious had gone to work and come up with an explosion.

This technique enables you to spot ideas
from the ordinary things that surround you

Once you use this list of ideas technique you'll begin to "key-in" hot new ideas from your environment—from things lying on your desk—from newspapers and magazines—from the simple things around you in your home. It gets the inner mind on the lookout for ideas. It tries to turn everything it comes across into grist for its mill.

Example: Some years ago when I was in advertising and using this technique for everything, I made up a list of ideas of ways in which we could make an advertising letter look different from an ordinary letter. Most advertising letters look monotonously alike—and the reason for this is that it's so difficult to come up with an idea that will make a letter look like something other than a letter and still have it something practical enough to mail.

I listed eight different "ideas" for getting a different-looking mailing, but it was pretty discouraging work. None of them seemed any good. But I had sweated out my list—and doing this work had gotten my aim across to the inner mind—the aim of finding an idea for a different-looking mailing. I wondered what "cerebration in depth" would do for me here. It did plenty.

My boss had just finished making up a special report for our company president. It was a five-page job, neatly typed on 8½ x 11 paper. It was stapled within a manila folder—with a label on the cover showing the subject of the report. It looked good—and it looked important. I saw it lying there on the boss's desk. My inner mind—which had been put on the alert when I made up my list—came flashing through and pounced on the report. Here was the idea I'd been looking for. Why not send out a letter that looked like this top-drawer report for the president? Much of our mail was sent to executives anyway and the idea seemed a natural. I wanted to try it out. Everyone but the boss said it was impracticable—that it would take forever—that it would cost too much.

We went ahead to test the idea. I had the letter printed on light tissue (ritzy-looking thin stuff like cigarette paper) —and to further the distinctive, confidential effect I used typewriter type and aloof-looking gray ink. We stapled these pages into a simulated black leather folder and cut a rectangular hole in the cover so the title of the report would show through. It looked like a million dollars. We mailed it flat in a large envelope. Here was a letter that looked like anything but a letter.

To test this new idea I used an old letter without changing a word—one we had been sending out in a mailing that looked just like any other mailing. The old letter in the ordinary-looking mailing was doing rather poorly. It was just about getting by. When we switched to the new presidential report format—using the same old letter word for word—the whole thing exploded, results went through the roof. We got six times as many orders as we needed to make a profit. We used this presidential report format for three years. It took that long for it to run down. It raised our department to a whole new level of profits.

The idea was based on something that's lying around in almost every office in America. But it was this list of ideas technique that enabled me to "key-in" something that was lying right under my nose. Strangely enough, these simple ideas that come from close at hand sources are often best—

but without this list of ideas technique to put you on the lookout for them you'll never know they're there.

Don't make this costly mistake

Don't make the costly mistake of thinking that ideas are something that only advertising men need. I used this list of ideas technique in the investment banking field—for the lecture platform—for writing books—as a salesman—and as a corporation executive. Ideas are the sparks that set off the fire of success in any undertaking, in any line of work. It's the idea that breathes the breath of life into a situation, that resurrects the whole project. Executives need them, teachers need them, secretaries need them. Every piece of successful activity you see going on about you is only somebody's idea in action.

Women can use this technique in dozens of ways

Women can use this list of ideas technique to go to town—to wake up any area of their lives. If a woman will sit down and write down all the ideas she can come up with for solving a specific problem, *by so doing* she can induce the inner mind to flash through and supply her the very ideas that she needs. She could, for example, find any one of the following lists paying off dramatically:

1. A list of ideas for finding a husband.
2. A list of ideas for modernizing her home.
3. A list of ideas for dressing with more distinction.
4. A list of ideas for helping her children (for example, Johnnie can't do his arithmetic).
5. A list of ideas for more interesting meals.

6. A list of ideas for improving relations with in-laws.
7. A list of ideas for making the evenings more stimulating.
8. A list of ideas for waking up a husband who's not aggressive enough in business.
9. A list of ideas for taking the pressure off a man who's under too much tension.

Any one of the above lists could be made up in a half-hour—and its benefits could be incalculable. Not only does this list of ideas technique prime the pump and often give you good ideas right off *while you're making up your list*—but, in cases where it doesn't, it can sow the seed for a humdinger of an idea to come through later on.

Don't make your lists too long

Remember that the purpose of these lists is to prime the pump, to get the inner mind started in flashing ideas on its own. I knew an author who wrote down 50,000 titles in an effort to find a good name for his book. *This is not the kind of thing we're talking about.* All we wish to do here is to make a small pump-priming investment—where, say, 30 minutes' work, will induce the inner mind to come through with a bonanza.

Specific examples of success

I have seen this technique transform droopy men and women into powerhouses. I have seen it quadruple one young man's income in a year. I have seen it promote a bookkeeper to the head accounting job in a large investment banking firm in a matter of months.

I have seen whole departments spring to life when the boss of the department started to use this technique. I have seen salesmen rise rapidly to the job of vice president in charge of sales through using this method of getting ideas. I have seen a girl stenographer in an advertising department start toying with these lists and become a good copywriter.

I have seen a young copywriter sit around for weeks—trying to come up with an advertising idea and getting nowhere—suddenly turn to this technique and on his second list of ideas come up with a haymaker. His bonanza headline read, "How to build a tax-free secondary income." Everybody wants a second income—and the thought of a tax-free second income simply made people drool.

I have seen what happened when I started to use this technique 20 years ago—how it brought me success in half a dozen different fields of activity—how it supplied me with 30 or 40 juicy ideas a year instead of the 3 or 4 I had been getting without it.

No matter what you want—the path to its rapid achievement lies in getting some hot ideas. This technique will give them to you. It will start the creative machinery turning within you—and turning out the ideas that will send an avalanche of power coursing through your life—making you the electric center of any group.

The next few pages are all worked out for you to make it simple for you to bring this dynamic technique into play.

Hints for Using This List of Ideas Technique

1. Choose an area in which you can use some good new ideas—for example—how to make profitable investments, how to get feeling better physically, how to give your company a good cost-cutting idea, how to do better in your daily job, how to quiet your nerves, how to wake up your life, how to find a good subject for a talk you must give, how to come in contact with more vital, more successful people.

2. Don't be discouraged if you have nothing to write down when you begin your list. Get a sheet of paper into your typewriter or pick up your pencil and write down anything, any thought on the subject that comes to you. You'll find that a half-hour session will result in a dozen items on your sheet of paper, and the chances are one of them will be a worthwhile idea.

3. When you look your list over—you may find that it looks pretty empty. This doesn't mean that it's wasted effort. You've taken the necessary steps to get your unconscious mind working on the problem. Even though there are no ideas on your current list which you can use, you've planted the seed and the ideas will come to you later.

4. Use this technique to set fire to any area of your life— to make you more alive, more successful. What you're really doing when you look for a hot idea is searching for an electric solution to some problem.

5. Don't think that an idea to be any good must be a whole new idea. Many ideas are variations of ideas already in use—and the idea you come up with may be a new angle to an old idea and will be a bonanza.

6. Remember that the few people who use this technique find the job of making up these lists of ideas a pain in the neck—but it pays off with a vengeance. It's dynamite.

On the next page is a sample
idea list all filled out.

SAMPLE IDEA LIST

Here is an idea list made up by a young husband
who wanted to get his life into high gear.

The purpose of this list of ideas is—

......*To find some good new ways to wake
up my business career—to get
my job progress off the ground.*

1. Subscribe to the U. S. News and World Report. (This will keep me in touch with the vital business news and whats going on in the world.)

2. Join an Executive Book Club. (This will bring me a book each month on some good executive subject.)

3. Have lunch with some new people. (The three or four fellows I lunch with everyday have been pretty much over each others minds.)

4. Start dressing like an executive. (Wear coat and pants to match.)

5. Think of myself as a $25,000. man. (It will help me to act like one.)

6. Stop wasting my time and strength in feeling animosity toward the unpleasant people around me—and swing that energy over into getting the things I want.

7. Try to figure out what my next job step up the ladder is and try to get ready for it!

8. Stop trying to show how fast I can come up with the answer and concentrate on arriving at the right answer.

Remember that you should use your best judgment
in choosing the best ideas from the list you make up.
This young man carried out three of the above ideas.
Which points on the list would you have favored?

*When you make up one of the above idea lists and find
nothing in it—the work is not lost. It lights a fuse
that brings explosive "illumination" later on.*

Blank form for making up your own list of ideas.

The purpose of this list of ideas is

_____

1. ....

2. ....

3. ....

4. ....

5. ....

6. ....

7. ....

8. ....

9. ....

10. ....

These lists can be made up at regular intervals. You might, for example, make up one 15-minute list a week. This will, on the average, give you one good idea a week—and one good new idea a week can make you terrific.

We're now ready for Action Two in this series— which will supply the mind with a whole new arsenal of "personalized" information it can use with electric force.

To supply you
with exciting new information
you can use
with breath-taking power

The purpose of this action is to supply your true self with special facts and insights that become thunder and lightning when the true self gets hold of them.

Here's the technique:

Each day for the next ten days clip out *one item* from a newspaper or magazine and paste it into the "scrapbook pages" supplied at the end of this chapter.

There are two rules to follow:

1. The items you choose must seem significant to you—they must catch your eye and your mind.

2. You must spend two minutes thinking about each item after you paste it into the book.

   (If you come across something in a book—which you can't cut out—then just copy off the item directly on to the "scrapbook" page.)

Why this is one of the hottest techniques a person can use

This technique will show you where your sharpest interests and your greatest powers lie. You'll quickly see that the items you choose have something in common—and that something is you. You'll get a clearer picture of the person you are—a new confirmation of the self. It will give you enormous help for achieving a dynamic, liberating fulfillment.

But great as that is—you'll get a second benefit that seems nothing short of a miracle

The items you clip out give your special talents the very tools they need to work with. They supply your mind with just the kind of material it needs to blaze into powerful action. Remember, *you* chose the articles *because* they have meaning to you—and you're equipped to use such "personalized" material with electric force.

The young man who woke up his life
with a "scrapbook"

This young man felt that he had capacities within him that he was hardly using at all. He wanted to feel the excitement of these powers in action. He was a pretty good friend of mine, and I wanted to help him if I could. I told him to try this "ten-day-scrapbook technique" for a starter.

He had a smallish job with a large corporation—an outfit that loomed pretty big in the financial field. Economics and the economic picture were big stuff in the life of this corporation. His own work did not touch directly on economics—but he was somewhat interested in it (and if he were going to get any place in the organization he'd have to know the subject).

He took my scrapbook suggestion. Each day for ten days he clipped from the newspaper (either the morning or the evening paper) something in this field that seemed hot to him. Then he pasted the item into his scrapbook— and then he spent a few minutes thinking about the item he had chosen.

This experiment worked out so excitingly well that we have decided to give you the whole dramatic story.

On the following pages is a repro-
duction showing the items he clipped
out.

Here are the first few items the young man clipped for his scrapbook:

NEW YORK WORLD-TELEGRAM AND SUN
SEPTEMBER 18

SONJ Head Hopeful Of Oil in North Sea

Associated Press

NEW ORLEANS, Sept. 18.— The head of the world's largest oil company believes prospects are bright for discovery of oil or gas in the North Sea.

"The North Sea really is a popular hunting ground these days," said M. J. Rathbone, board chairman of the Standard Oil Co. (New Jersey). "The area today looks like Libya about five years ago.

Rathbone made his remarks yesterday at a news conference after speaking at the final session of the annual meeting of the Independent Natural Gas Assn. of America.

He said Jersey Standard is one of about 20 companies currently conducting geophysical explorations in the North Sea.

NEW YORK HERALD-TRIBUNE, SEPT. 24

Autos

(Indicator? The first 1964 models in the showrooms touched off a buyer response that would gladden the heart and pocketbook of any auto maker. In this case, Chrysler was the happy manufacturer with the initial entries in the 1964 auto market race. In two days last week, it sold 11,490 new Chryslers and Plymouths. A year earlier, the Chrysler division took 10 days to sell 19,109 new models. *The buying climate appears to be on the level of the 1955 model year, which was the greatest in the history of the industry," an executive observed with elation.*

NEW YORK WORLD-TELEGRAM AND SUN
SEPTEMBER 26

Shares listed on the New York Stock Exchange have passed the 8 billion mark, the Exchange announced today.

The Exchange estimates that the 8 billion milestone was reached with the start of trading yesterday in 1,479,725 additional common shares of ACF Industries Inc., issued in a 2-for-1 split of the manufacturing company's stock.

The Big Board's list has about doubled since 1956, both in number of shares and market value. Since reaching 4 billion in March, 1956, shares listed have increased at an average rate of about one billion every two years. The latest billion was added in the 22-month period since November, 1961.

Market value—computed at $224 billion in March, 1956—passed the $400 billion point last month.

NEW YORK HERALD-TRIBUNE, SEPTEMBER 25

The world's population explosion, unchecked and untouched by modern scientific and technological developments, is getting to be far more menacing to the survival of mankind than any other event of history.

That's the sum and substance of a massive (680 pages), analytical study prepared by the United Nations Demographic and Social Statistical Section and entitled Demographic Yearbook, 1962.

Consider, for a moment, the following facts of the population bulge:

In mid-1961 the world population was approximately 3,069 billion.

—During the decade of the '50s, the population increased by 560 million, which is greater than the total population of India.

—Since 1960 the bulge was bigger by another 61 million, or an annual increase equivalent to three times the population of Argentina or one-third that of the United States.

The UN study shows that between 1950 and 1961 the annual rate of the "explosion" was at 1.8 per cent, but during the latter part of the same period the pace quickened, reaching 2 per cent between 1960 and 1961.

There are now 23 persons for each square kilometer of land in the world, compared with 18 ten years ago.

NEW YORK WORLD-TELEGRAM AND SUN
SEPTEMBER 21

Natural Gas Business Sees Booming Future

Associated Press

WASHINGTON, Sept. 21.—Until and if the United States runs out of gas, no end to the growth of the natural gas business—a dramatic chapter in the nation's industrial history —appears in sight.

When oil producers started harnessing the gas that blew out of wells drilled for oil, a giant new industry was born. Some wells had been drilled mainly for gas, but it wasn't until oil operations . started capturing the gas from their wells, instead of letting it go to waste, that the natural gas industry really got going.

NEW YORK HERALD-TRIBUNE, SEPT. 17

¶Rides. Canadian Pacific Railway announced plans early yesterday to cut passenger fares beginning Oct. 27 in a move to halt the continuing decline in passenger revenues. Details will be announced later, the privately - owned carrier said. Next, the government - owned Canadian National Railways said it would introduce new services and cut fares by up to 58 per cent, starting Oct. 27.

NEW YORK HERALD-TRIBUNE, SEPT. 19

Aussies Shuck Royal for Dollar

CANBERRA.

Australia's new decimal currency will be headed by the "dollar," Harold Holt, the Treasury Minister, announced yesterday. This reverses the June decision to use the name "Royal" for the new currency units.

Mr. Holt said the government had not selected "dollar" originally because it would not be a distinctive Australian name but there was now clearly a major body of opinion in favor of it. Serious consideration had been given to "pound" but there would have been technical difficulties in introducing a new unit with the same name as the old but only half its value.

Australia hopes to introduce decimal currency by February, 1966.

NEW YORK HERALD-TRIBUNE
SEPTEMBER 22

¶Prices. Companies were busy marking up prices and catching up with competitors who had already marked up theirs. The steel industry was caught in a price parade when Jones & Laughlin, fifth largest steel producer, lifted prices of most lines of oil country tubular goods about 4 per cent. Next came U. S. Steel, followed quickly by five other companies. In New York, lead moved up ¼ cent a point to 11¾ cents, the seventh price increase since November. One of the major textile manufacturers, Cannon Mills, Inc., announced increases of 2 per cent in terry cloth prices. Retail prices, however, will not be affected until mid-1964. *Over-all, the price boosts did not appear dangerous enough to stir fears of inflation. Economists put the movements down as the stirring of a normal economy.*

NEW YORK HERALD-TRIBUNE, SEPT. 23

PRE-CLIPPING THE PRESS: When Fortune arrives in the mails tomorrow it'll report that merchants are more optimistic about the next few months' prospects than they have been in years. For '64 auto dealers are very bullish, all home-goods merchants in this semi-annual survey look for a 6 per cent hike in volume. Clothing retailers see a 5 per cent increase. . . . Fortune's economists say builders think apartment-building will hit an annual rate of 550,000 family units this year

The young man speaks up

One morning after he had been on this "scrapbook" for just a week he attended an executive meeting in the company he worked for. When the discussion got around to economics and finance he sensed a new confidence. He felt sure of his ground—*and mind you he had clipped just seven items thus far*. He had never spoken up in any of these meetings before—but this time he quietly made a few observations about the economic picture. He had something to say on the "population explosion," which was then much in the news. He pointed out a new way this would affect the company. People looked at him—wondered how come.

He told me it was the scrapbook. He had read the newspapers intelligently before—but now, choosing the items that interested him—then pasting them into his scrapbook —and then thinking about them for a few minutes—gave him powerful new tools to work with. Now he had the facts he needed right at his fingertips—now he had some worthwhile comment to make. He had done some thinking about the items. He had something vital to say.

The car pool defers to him

The same thing happened in the car pool in which he travelled each day. He quickly became the one to whom others looked for information and opinion. He played it quietly—didn't try to get over into topics on which he hadn't clipped anything—never tried to go beyond the point where his thinking on a subject had stopped.

This man found that in ten days he had become a different person to other people and to himself—and he had used this scrapbook technique just for business. It works on a larger scale when you clip anything that interests you on *any* subject—and of course the longer you keep a general scrapbook the greater its force in helping you find yourself and the greater the supply of vital "electrically personalized" facts, ideas and insights it gives you to work with.

But you've got to clip and paste

When you clip out something and paste it into your scrapbook, in a very real sense you make it yours. The very act of clipping an item and pasting it into your book *fastens it in your mind*. But what usually happens with items in print that interest us? We give them a passing nod of recognition as we hear them "ring the bell of meaning" within us—and then they are usually lost to us forever. They soon get swallowed up in the thousands and thousands of impressions that keep streaming into our lives. We must stop letting this precious material slip through our fingers—and we must stop it at once.

Use this technique now

You don't have to go out and buy a scrapbook first. Use the two pages at the end of this chapter for your "get started scrapbook." The point of this whole book—here as in every other action it recommends—is to give you just what you need to get started on these key actions that will throw open the floodgates of life. Everything you need is supplied. Once you try the scrapbook idea for ten days you'll soon enough get yourself a full-size scrapbook. You'll never want to be without the enormous help this technique provides for vital, vigorous, meaningful living. The main thing is to get started. Clip and paste in one item today—anything that interests you.

The young lady was scornful of the scrapbook idea

I suggested to a young lady that she keep a scrapbook. She was scornful of it. She told me:

"There's nothing new about a scrapbook. We used to keep them all the time when we were kids. I still have mine which I filled up when I was eight or nine years old."

No, there's nothing new about it. What is new, I think, is showing the enormous power there is in it—the way it can help you find yourself, and the way it skyrockets your effectiveness by giving you all new material to work with—and not just new material, but material that "is made for you"—material you've chosen because you're you—material you're equipped by your very nature to use. It throws open the door to a whole new level of dynamic action.

What happens when you feed them to your scrapbook?

When you paste these items into your scrapbook a seeming miracle takes place. The information they contain, the ideas they suggest, the insights they give are now *added to you*—and once they are added to you their voltage is enormously stepped up.

The item that caught your eye is no longer the same item it would be to somebody else. Your system now processes the items you have selected and multiplies their power potential. Your scrapbook becomes a powerhouse—ready any time you throw the switch—to fortify you with this "personalized" material which your inner self has magnified in power.

Below is a diagram which shows what happens when you choose—say, ten scrapbook items—from among a couple of hundred things you read:

Each tab around the frame represents
an item you skimmed—some 200 in all.

This diagram shows how ten items out of 200 caught your eye.

The ten items show where your real interests lie.

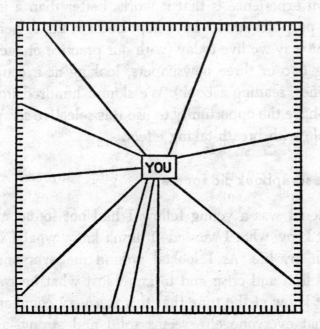

YOU

You then feed the ten magnetic items into your scrapbook.

Many great persons have used this technique

Many great persons have used a similar technique—the technique out of which their greatness came. They kept diaries, or journals, as they called them. In these journals they put down their thoughts on the things they came across—and recorded the thoughts which came to them. If you can keep a journal in this fine old sense, then by all means keep one—but probably not one person in a hundred keeps such a journal—or is likely to.

Here is where the magic of the scrapbook comes in. It gives you much the same power as a journal—but with a tenth of the effort—and takes only a tenth of the time. My own experience is that it works better than a journal for my purposes—and I have kept both. It fits in perfectly with the way we live today (with our practice of each day reading two or three newspapers, looking at a couple of magazines, reading a book). We skim a hundred items in a day—have the opportunity to use this selective scrapbook principle with breath-taking effect.

What a scrapbook did for me

When I was a young fellow I had not found myself. I didn't know what I wanted—I didn't know what I should do with my life. As I looked around me everyone else seemed firm and crisp and to know just what he wanted. I didn't know at the time that this is a very common illusion—that everyone else seems solid and strong—and to ourselves we seem weak. The thought used to make me feel pretty low. I felt as though I were attached to nothing —insubstantial—floating around in the air—if floating around can be used to describe a person who feels generally unhappy.

The scrapbook changed everything for me. I kept it for a year. It gave edge and shape and meaning to my existence. I began to see what I wanted—the direction my life should take. Everything pointed to some kind of teaching—or writing—or public speaking—with my specialty being a kind of popularized treatment of techniques for living.

But important as this knowledge I gained about myself proved to be—equally important was the new power I gained through using the information contained in the items I had selected for my scrapbook. They were a gold mine—information I was able to use with telling effect because it was mine in a very special sense. I had an electric battery of 400 items whose power I could tap at any time. No matter what group I was working with I had something to contribute on almost any subject that came up. It's amazing how a person can use 400 items which he has chosen because they have special significance to him—and not only did I have the 400 items themselves to call on—but these 400 could be used in combination with each other—and here the possibilities are endless.

The scrapbook is mental capital

Whenever I had an hour in the evening I would pull out the scrapbook and go through it—refreshing my mind on the facts, the ideas, the insights in each item. I got so

I knew my scrapbook by heart (as far as the hot central point of each item was concerned).

If any person is a poor conversationalist—is ever at a loss to know what to talk about—let him keep a scrapbook. He'll always have interesting facts, penetrating insights, exciting ideas on tap—information he knows how to use with incisive brilliance because it is his own.

Your own idea of yourself

What a person thinks of himself is of course the thing that matters most—and here is where the scrapbook does its most powerful work. It makes you a special person in your own eyes. And you are a special person—but so few of us ever get the feeling of our own "specialness" and get it right. We must remember that our own good estimate of ourselves depends in part on the feeling that the things we know are of real significance—and a scrapbook gives us a great fund of information that is highly significant to us. (We chose it *because* of that significance.) A scrapbook is thus able to give us a solid sense of inner worth. Here is a new source of strength and confidence. We now have, of all things, a scrapbook behind us.

Who should keep a scrapbook?

This dynamo works its power for everyone. A housewife can use it for keeping all kinds of items in reference to her home. It will enable her to build a household that's a model of charm and grace—and not just charm and grace in general—but a special kind of charm and grace that are an expression of her real self.

A young man uses a scrapbook in connection with his

work, and he's one of the best-informed men in the company. He shines when he appears before the big shots. They are amazed at the fertility of his mind—the pertinent facts he has always on tap—the way he is able to put his thoughts across. Most of us so often feel left out of things —that we have nothing to say on the matter before us. But this man has something good and something to the point on almost every subject that comes up. The people he works with don't know about the scrapbook. They think he's a genius. He's not. He's just an able young man who follows the practice of clipping items that have meaning to him and his job. He pastes them in his book—thinks a few minutes about each one—and from then on they are his for immediate dynamic use any time he needs them.

A teacher uses a scrapbook on everything related to her job. It has made her one of the most effective teachers in the whole school. Her teaching is alive. The children are co-operative, interested and excited.

A general—or a special—scrapbook?

What kind of scrapbook should you keep? Should it be a general one in which you paste any item that interests you, or should it be for one special subject? I recommend a general scrapbook in which you keep anything that "catches your mind."

Thus you will get coverage on the special subjects, too. And with a general book you get the powerful help it gives you in finding the real self. It can lead you into a life of ever-increasingly meaningful activity. But if you've already found yourself, if the die is pretty well cast, if you know what you're after and you're pursuing it—then, if you insist, keep a special collection of items that deal with your special subject. It will enormously increase your effectiveness in any specific area. For example, a scrapbook related to your job can literally multiply your power in a matter of days.

I've started my scrapbook again

When I look back and see how for years I leaned on those 400 items in my scrapbook, it makes me wonder how I ever let myself drop this terrific technique. I told myself I was too busy—and maybe I thought the big job that a scrapbook was to accomplish for me had already been achieved. It had helped me find myself—it had made me effective in my work—it had given me a solid foundation on which to stand.

But a few months ago I started keeping a general scrapbook again—and I can feel a new surge of life—a new dynamic—as my mind is given all this fresh "personalized" material to go to work on. One item alone has given me an idea for a great new project for giving young men and women the help that they need right where they need it. And I can feel a new stepping-up of confidence as this arsenal of material gathers at my back.

Great men and fools

It is said that great men and fools keep diaries—and perhaps this can be paraphrased to read "great men and fools keep scrapbooks." But this I know—that every person has a spark of greatness in him—and the saddest thing of all is to live one's life without ever having that spark burst forth into flame.

Use this scrapbook technique for ten days—and you can start the exciting process that will define yourself to yourself—that will supply your mind with rich new material it knows how to use with telling brilliance—that will give you a new feeling of strength as this arsenal of "personalized information" gathers at your back.

What to do

For the next ten days—cut out each day from a newspaper or magazine some item that has special significance to you—and paste it in the "scrapbook" at the end of this chapter.

Hints for using this technique
are given on the following page.

Scrapbook Hints

1. Choose items that have special interest to you. That's the only criterion.

2. The items you choose will give you excellent hints as to where your real strength lies.

3. Choose at least one scrapbook item a day for ten days.

4. If you come across something in a book that attracts you —copy the quote directly on to the scrapbook page.

5. You'll feel new confidence as all this material gathers— ready to assist you at the drop of a hat.

6. This technique gives you the rough equivalent of the great man's journal—with one tenth the effort.

7. The act of clipping and pasting—and then thinking for a few minutes about each item—makes it yours to use with power.

8. A scrapbook gives you special facts to use—it gives you special ideas—it gives you special insights—special, because the material you choose has special meaning to you.

Put ten items on the next two
pages in the next ten days.

Ten-Day Get Started Scrapbook

(Paste items in square below.)

*Underline the salient portions of each item—and circle
the heart of the item.*

Ten-Day Get Started Scrapbook

(Paste items in square below.)

Think about each item for two minutes after pasting.

To strengthen
your judgment enormously

The purpose of this action is to increase your judgment *immediately and dramatically.*

Here's the technique:

> Whenever you face a situation on which you must form a judgment—write down all the factors you can think of that affect the decision. (Handy forms for doing this are supplied at the end of the chapter.)

What do we mean by forming judgments?

When a person forms a judgment he decides which of the various courses of action open to him it would be most advantageous to pursue.

Example: A man with a $9,000 job has been offered a

$12,000 job with another company. He doesn't know whether to take the new job or keep the old one. To make this decision calls for the forming of a judgment.

He should turn at once to this "list of factors" technique

If the man has any doubt about what his decision should be, he should immediately jot down all the factors he can think of that enter into it. Things like this:

1. New job means $3,000 more a year.
2. I'd sacrifice ten years seniority in present job.
3. Most of my pension would be lost.
4. New job means a better private office and a secretary.
5. New job sounds more "ulcerish."
6. I'm now at my pay ceiling in present job.
7. I'm now 40 and don't want to make a mistake.
8. But I guess it's now or never.
9. I like the crowd I now work with—don't know new bunch.
10. New company is faster growing.
etc., etc.

A list—of, say, 20 factors like this which he should consider—will do more to help him reach a wise decision than any other one thing he can do. This technique as a means of forming judgments (making decisions) is nothing short of electric.

Instances of where to use this technique

It can be used—for example—

(a) By a husband and wife to decide whether to build an extension on their present home (family is increasing) or whether to buy a larger home.

(b) It can be used by a mother in deciding the best way to handle Johnnie, who "won't finish his school work"—whether to promise him a reward or to threaten to punish him.

(c) It can be used by an "exurbanite" to decide whether to buy a tractor and cut his 25 acres of "lawn" himself or to hire a man with his own tractor to do it.

(d) It can be used by an executive to decide whether to drop an old product on which sales are running out—or to try to get some more mileage out of it.

The young man with weak judgment

A few years ago I worked in a business office; one day a young man came to me and asked me how he could improve his judgment. He said that judgment seemed to be his weak point. Then he added with an apologetic little laugh:

"I guess I need to learn how to think."

I told him he didn't have to learn to think. Everybody knows how to think. Our minds know how to proceed. The job is to get them to proceed.

But he still wasn't satisfied. He came right back at me with:

"If I know how to think, then why don't I? You make it sound as though thinking were the most natural thing in the world. But it's common knowledge that people do little thinking. They avoid it like poison."

"Of course they do! At least most of them do. But the

reason people avoid thought is *not* that they don't know how to think—but because formidable hurdles stand in the way of getting themselves to think."

Then I told him about this "list of factors" technique and what a powerful catapult it is for getting us over those hurdles.

One reason we hate to think

One reason we hate to think and make decisions is that it demands attention to the topic in hand.

One of the biggest stumbling blocks to good judgment is that forming judgments means giving our attention to the topic before us—and our attention wants to wander. Our attention span is pitifully short. Listen to what the great William James says about "attention":

> There is no such thing as voluntary attention sustained for more than a few seconds at a time. [and] What is called sustained voluntary attention is a repetition of successive efforts which bring back the topic to the mind.

The attention is like a puppy on a leash—and wants forever to turn to something new. We keep calling our minds back to the topic, but it's hard work and most of us soon get enough of it.

One evening recently I tried to form a judgment on a simple situation—the kind of thing all of us face all the time: whether to make a special trip into the city the following morning to take care of some business that was long overdue—or whether to run the risk of letting the business go until the following week when I was going into the city anyway. I hoped to kill two birds with one stone and save myself the extra trip.

I sat at the kitchen table trying to think my way through to a decision. Every few seconds my mind tried to escape to something new. I had to keep yanking it back. I found myself reaching out for an apple that was in a bowl on the table and examining it. I put the apple back and forced my attention back to the decision I was trying to make.

A few seconds later I started snapping in and out the point of my ball-point pen. I then noticed there was some fuzz on the point and I stopped to wipe it off. Again I yanked my attention back to the topic. A few seconds later my mind seemed to hit a blank spot and I thought of nothing at all.

Then I called my attention back from nowhere and went on trying to fight this ceaseless battle with a wandering attention. Then I took my pen and made up a "list of factors," and with this technique I had my decision in a few minutes. The trip to the city could wait.

How this list of factors "outsmarts" the mind

Bear in mind that the very essence of forming judgments is a question of *keeping the mind on a given topic—*and bear in mind that the *mind doesn't like this.* It wants always to turn its attention to something new. And here is where this "list of factors" technique comes through to save the day. It outsmarts the mind. It plays along with the mind's "weakness" for wanting forever to turn to something new. It *caters* to the mind's wish to turn from one thing to another. It gives the mind many different factors to move about in—*but all of them are within the topic you want the mind to stay on.*

Here is a perfect set-up for the forming of judgments—with the attention more or less captive. The mind can weigh the various factors individually and consider the interrelation of each factor with the others. The list of factors encourages the mind to keep turning the topic over and looking at it from all sides. It fosters the discovery of new factors in the process, and the discovery of these new factors stimulates attention—keeps it vibrantly alive.

This is the kind of work that the mind knows how to handle if it will only give its attention to it—and the whole point, of course, is that with this technique you find it infinitely simpler to make the mind give it that attention.

To try to handle decisions—to try to form judgments on sticky situations—without some kind of written list like this is like trying to multiply something like 86 times 47 in your head. You can get so you can handle it, but it's infinitely simpler with pencil and paper.

This technique gives a "non-thinker" judgment

A 45-year-old man with an imaginative, creative mind never bothered to do any of the hard "attention-thinking" that must go into the forming of difficult judgments. He encouraged himself to believe that his ability to come up with good ideas excused him from the necessity of developing anything so pedestrian as good judgment.

This man seemed to have no capacity for mental work that required attention-effort. He thought of himself as an intuitive thinker. He wouldn't even bother to evaluate the ideas he came up with. (He'd do the creative work—let others put in the brain sweat.)

This man's boss was one of the most brilliant and one of the wisest men I ever knew. He knew that the "idea man" would be infinitely more valuable to him if he could get him to use his head—if he could get him to knuckle down to an occasional bout of hard concentrated thought. The boss was pretty sure that this man's judgment was just as good as anybody else's—if he would only exercise some mental discipline—not be so lazy.

One day the boss called him in and asked him for some help. He told him:

"We've got to decide the best way of handling the XYZ account and it's a tough decision. You know more about this account than anyone in the office—and I wonder if you will jot down a list of factors for me to consider when I try to work the thing out."

The "idea man" came back in an hour with a list of 14 factors he thought should be taken into account. He and the boss looked it over, and the boss thanked him for doing such a fine job with the list. And then he threw him a challenge.

"Look, Ralph. Will you give me a hand with this thing? I've got a couple of big rush jobs to worry about this weekend. Will you take this list home and try to figure out what we should do about it?"

Ralph said O.K.—and the boss had a pretty good idea of what would happen. He knew that there wouldn't be anything very wrong with Ralph's judgment as long as he had the list to help him. But he didn't know just how good Ralph's judgment would be. On Monday morning Ralph came in with a honey of a memo—a memo that made a clean-cut recommendation of just what to do about the account—and gave a masterful analysis to support his recommendation.

This list of factors technique eventually developed the "non-thinking" Ralph into one of the soundest judgments in the company. He's now consulted by the bosses on all kinds of problems. The list of factors idea (which he got from the boss) was just the thing he needed.

This technique gives a person courage to make decisions

Many people are scared to death when they have to make a decision. This keeps them from exercising good judgment and it keeps them from making decisions on time—when they're needed. Anyone who has worked in a large organization knows how few people in it are willing to make decisions and accept responsibility for them—even when the decisions are part of their jobs.

It was a certain man's job to order raw materials for the factory and keep them in stock. Whenever the inventory fell below a certain level, the stock room would send him a form with the name of the material on it—and he was supposed to use his judgment in deciding how many tons should be ordered and put the order right through.

But the poor guy could never make up his mind how much to order. He couldn't decide whether to order two tons or ten tons. If he ordered two tons the price per pound was higher. If he ordered ten tons he made a substantial saving per pound, but the sale of the product might dry up and then they'd have tons of material left over.

The form to be filled out would lie on his desk waiting for him to get up his courage—but he seemed constitutionally unable to make up his mind—to fill it out, sign it, and send it through.

He wouldn't act until he had to—till the phones started

ringing—till material was nearly out of stock and he had to take action. Such timidity is rife in business. And I know how real it is. Once a year I had to put through an order of how many books to print and I hated to face it.

But here the "list of factors" technique is a lifesaver. It gives the anxious man a point around which to marshal his courage. It gives him something tangible to do. As soon as we have picked up the pad and pencil we have faced the situation—and as soon as we have faced the situation we have stopped running away—and when we stop running away we are less afraid.

Touching all bases

One of the reasons we are uneasy about making decisions is that we are haunted by the fear that we might miss some factor that's the heart of the whole business— that we may be overlooking something that will cause us to make a real boner—that we'll not only show poor judgment but that we'll look utterly ridiculous.

A woman in a church was once given the authority to decide what should happen to a lot of old Bibles that the church was finished with. She was a kind-hearted lady, filled with Christian good will—and she wanted the Bibles to go where they would do the most good. She decided to send them to the Armenians. She completely overlooked the fact that the Bibles were in English and the Armenians wouldn't be able to read them.

Whenever I have a judgment to make, this business of sending English Bibles to the Armenians is somewhere at the back of my mind. I have the uneasy feeling that I might come up with a boner as beautiful as that.

But this list of factors technique is a wonder here, too.

Not only does the tangible presence of a written list help to dispel this anxiety—but it tends to make such boners less likely. When you begin to list all the factors you can think of, it invites the mind to come through with all the big ones anyway. This technique is a powerful ally in seeing that you touch all bases.

The list of factors technique pushes through decisions that are ready to be made

For a long while I had been trying to make a decision as to what subject my next book should deal with. Would it be something in the executive field—or something in the popularized-philosophy field, something like the wisdom of living "here and now"?

I was carrying around the weight of this unmade decision. I had thought of it on and off for months—but had never sat down and made up my list of factors.

Here is where the technique can give you dramatic help in a matter of seconds—as I soon found out. I picked up a pencil and began to write down points in rapid-fire sequence. By the time I had gotten to point nine (in about 90 seconds), I had my decision.

Many of us are going around thinking we have difficult decisions still to be made—carrying around this burden on our backs when we needn't. The decision is there waiting for us. All we have to do is ask for it—and the way to ask for it is to start writing down a list of factors that enter into the decision. Try it. It clears the decks of your mind of decisions that are already made—or which are so nearly made that all they need is this nudge to push them over into a made decision.

Improve your judgment. It's the path to strength

A person of good judgment has an aura of strength about him—and you can immediately feel that strength. As soon as you develop it people will know it and want to avail themselves of it. What most people need is not more conventional education—but to get so they can form good judgments—make wise decisions. Here is strength—satisfaction—success.

This technique is a powerhouse

This technique is a dynamic aid in forming good judgments. It overcomes the greatest hindrance to thought—the mind's short attention span and its desire to turn ever to something new. It capitalizes on this very weakness. It enables anyone to start turning out good judgments, making sound decisions. It's a bonanza to anyone who's timid about making decisions. It lessens the fear that we have not touched all bases—and lessens the chance of our not doing so. It shows us that many decisions that still weigh us down have already been made.

Remember that you don't have to learn how to think. But you do have to do something about getting over the hurdles that stand in the way of your thinking. This technique is a honey for that purpose. It lets you do the kind of "attention-thinking" on which sound judgment is based. It enables you to weigh the factors that enter into a judgment and to see the interrelation of those factors.

This is something the mind knows how to do. It knows how to take the factors properly into account and come up with a decision—if it can only get to think—and with this technique it can get to think—steadily and strong.

Hints for Using This Technique

1. Judgment is the answer to strength—and this technique is the path to judgment.

2. The problem is how to keep the attention on the matter to be judged.

3. This technique capitalizes on the mind's desire to turn forever to something new. It gives the mind a list of factors for it to move about in—but all the factors are on the subject you want the mind to consider.

4. Put in your list every factor you can think of that affects the decision.

5. Go over your list. Turn the topic this way and that. See it from all sides.

6. The mind knows how to weigh these factors, see their interrelation.

7. Use this technique wherever there's a difficult judgment to be formed.

On the next page is a sample "list of factors" a couple used to see if they should build an addition to their present home or buy a larger home.

Sample "list of factors" as filled in by a husband and wife.

The decision to be made—

**Whether to build on to our present house
or buy a larger house.**

Background story:

This couple needs more room. They have to decide whether to build an addition to their present home or buy another home. An older home in a better suburban section is up for sale. It's the size home they need.

Here is their list of factors:

1. If we build on to present home it will crowd the lot.
2. Present house would be O.K. with two more rooms.
3. Our present neighbors leave something to be desired.
4. We now have three noisy dogs close by.
5. Car pool would be out for husband—he'd have to travel by train.
6. We'd need two cars instead of one—a jalopy to take to the station.
7. Husband finds present neighborhood depressing.
8. Our 2 children would have to switch schools.
9. Addition to present house would cost about $8,000.
10. New house would cost $8,000 and our present house.
11. People in other section are quieter.
12. Present neighborhood is getting worse.
13. Taxes would be $300 a year more in better section.
14. Kitchen equipment in present home needs replacement.
15. We'd get a lift out of moving to better neighborhood.
16. There would be more work around the place for husband if we move.

Their decision is on next page.

The decision—

As soon as they got their list of factors down on paper and looked it over, the husband and wife looked knowingly at each other. It showed them clearly what they were thinking. They wanted to get out of the neighborhood.

They had a buyer for their home—so there would be no trouble there. But there were two big considerations. The children would have to change schools. One was happy where he was. One was unhappy. There didn't seem to be much risk there. The end of the term was in sight anyway—and they would wait for that.

But the new place would cost them a bit more to run. Taxes were higher. They would need a jalopy—and need to insure it. The railroad commuting would cost more than the car pool. They figured it would cost them around a thousand dollars more a year to live in the new set-up.

And they figured it was worth it—that they could swing it with a little care and figuring. They decided to move.

Form for your use.

This form is for jotting down your list of factors.

The decision to be made ....

....

Factors to be considered:

1. ....
2. ....
3. ....
4. ....
5. ....
6. ....
7. ....
8. ....
9. ....
10. ....
11. ....
12. ....
13. ....
14. ....
15. ....

Consider the decision from all angles—keep rolling the thing over—going from one factor to another. If in the process you see a new factor, put it down.

Now we're ready for Part IV of this book's great new program of action for victorious living—

Three powerful actions to open the flood-gates of material success.

PART IV

HOW TO INCREASE
YOUR WEALTH

This part of the book is the prizewinner—alive with
wealth-creating action. It shows how to switch on three mighty
dynamos and set your life humming with healthy fortune-build-
ing power.

Here are the three great actions—

Action 1

This is the simplest action in the book—all you do is
ask yourself one question every time you're about to
spend any money. It whips your scattered forces into
line, channels them into a healthy "money drive,"
gives you the one indispensable quality to financial
success.

Action 2

This action ties you in at once with the irresistible
power of a universal law—a law so strong it insures the

financial success of anyone who obeys it. This law is psychologically sound as a rock—and the most reasonable and most pragmatic of all laws.

Action 3

This action steps up dramatically the size of the financial aspirations your mind is able to envision—and it steps up concurrently the power you need to achieve these greater aims. Here is the answer not only to Thinking Big but to Doing Big.

The creation of wealth follows certain definite laws. Get the surging power of these great laws at your back. You were meant to be rich. Let them make you so.

Now let's turn to these three exciting
actions for building material prosperity.

To give you
"financial drive"

The purpose of this action is swiftly to build up the drive you need to earn large income—to accumulate wealth.

Here's the technique:

Every time you spend any money—whether it's a nickel or a large amount of money—ask yourself this question:

"Will this expenditure further me in reaching my financial goal?"

I suggested this technique to a young man who said he wanted to accumulate some money. (The figure he had set for himself was, for some reason he did not divulge to me, a nice round quarter of a million dollars.) He complained that he had gotten nowhere with his goal. He smiled at my suggestion.

"Do you mean to tell me that every time I spend a nickel for a newspaper I should ask myself, 'Is this purchase going to help me reach my financial goal?'"

"Yes, you should."

He said it sounded too trivial for him. I told him there's a lot more to it than meets the eye—that the purpose of asking the question is not simply to decide whether to spend or save the nickel—that the explosive power in this technique is this:

> It brings you up sharp a dozen times a day, makes you mentally picture your goal, makes you continually face the big question of whether you're going after it, whether you're investing your money *and* your time *and* your energy in getting what you say you're out to get.

This young man was dissatisfied—fed up. He said he wanted financial success, but he guessed his trouble was that he really lacked drive. This is the most common of all situations. Despite all you hear about how acquisitive everyone is, how much everyone wants financial success, my guess is that not one person in 50 is really acquisitive—really *wants* a money success.

The trouble with many people is simply this: They'd like very much to have a money success—they want it enough so they'll never be satisfied without it—but they don't want it enough to go out and get it. They lack money drive.

Do you want money? Do you want dollar success? If

your answer is yes—then you've got to give yourself to it. When a farmer wants a crop of corn he plants corn—when he wants a crop of potatoes he plants potatoes. If you want a dollar crop then you have to plant the seeds of financial success.

Immediate help through this technique

This technique will start at once to build "financial drive"—it will start at once to increase your cash on hand. You'll be cash ahead the first day you try it—but this immediate gain (maybe just a nickel, or a quarter) is just a token of the river of plenty this technique can set free. This technique reminds you continuously of your goal—prunes away all trivial pursuits—gathers up your scattered forces and unifies them—channels your strength into your main goals—heads you toward a dollar success—gives you financial drive.

The $2,000 expense

Here is an exciting example of this technique in action. At my suggestion a 30-year-old man began to use this technique—started to ask the question every time he spent anything, "Will this expenditure further my financial goal?"

The first day he was 40 cents ahead—the second day he saved a dollar and a quarter. He was rather hard up and these savings helped—but the big thing was the change that began to take place in him as he asked himself this question a dozen times a day. It dramatically changed his attitude. It dramatically changed his life.

The big corporation he worked for paid him $5,500 a year as a "management trainee." He was chosen as a trainee because of the unusually high score he got on his intelligence test and in spite of the fact that he had no college degree. (He had had only three years of college.)

As a "trainee" he had the chance to become a big shot in the company—if everything worked out well—but things weren't working out too well for him. Every time an opening developed a trainee was moved up—but it was always someone else. They were moving up the men who had college degrees—fellows with less brains and less ability than he. He soon saw what the score was—no college degree, no promotion.

This young fellow was a nut about cars. He was considering turning his car in for a bucket-seat convertible—and he had just about made up his mind to do so—but he had not reckoned on the power of this technique. He had been using this technique for a couple of weeks—asking himself the pointed question every time he spent any money.

It had begun to do things to him. It brought him continually face to face with the big central question of his life. It was backing him into a corner where he couldn't escape. He couldn't kid himself any longer.

When he asked himself the big question, "Will this $2,000 spent for a car further my financial goal?" he knew the jig was up. As soon as he faced the question in this way he saw clearly what he should do. He should spend the $2,000—and three nights a week—getting his degree in Business Administration.

The decision pays off fast

He was ready to wait two years—if necessary—for his decision to bear fruit—but this technique had already begun to develop financial drive within him. It was making him ambitious, forceful—and he decided to have a hand in influencing how long it would be necessary to wait. He'd take action to get himself moved up *before* he earned his degree.

He went to his boss—told him he was working on his degree—made out a strong case for himself—reminded the boss of the high score he had gotten on his intelligence test—gave him facts and figures to show how well he was handling his current job. He was quiet, courteous—but strong.

The boss was a little taken aback by this new show of force from someone whom he had rated as more docile— and the boss knew from experience that forceful young men were apt to leave the company and go with its competitors if they didn't get what they wanted.

The young man was given the next good opening that came along—a good spot in the middle executive group. His income was immediately upped. He had changed from a boy to a man in a matter of weeks—and the whole thing had gotten started when he was about to buy a magazine one day and had asked himself what the purchase would contribute to his financial success.

Where do you eat lunch and with whom?

When I began my business career as a clerk in Wall Street I used to go out to lunch every day with some of the fellows who worked in the same department with me. After lunch we'd stand around the entrance to the building —indulging in idle chatter—waiting like schoolboys for the time when we'd have to go back inside. One of the older men in the company with whom I'd grown friendly spoke to me about it. He suggested that if I had any idea of becoming somebody in the company I was doing exactly the wrong thing in hanging around the entrance to the building with the other clerks.

"Invest your lunch hour in your career!"

"Do you mean I should study a book on finance—or something like that?"

"No, I don't mean that. Go out to lunch with someone who can stimulate you. Invest your lunch hour in your success. When you have lunch with the same people you work with all day long it does nothing for you. If you must eat lunch with the boys, then for heaven's sake don't come back and hang around the entrance to the building with them. It makes you 'one of the kids'—and my guess is that you have something more in mind."

I decided to make my lunch hour count—to invest it in success. I screwed up my courage and asked the company's star salesman to have lunch with me. I was making $40 a week. He was making $60,000 a year. He was much more than just a good salesman. He was a big man in the company—smart as a whip—with excellent judgment—was greatly respected by everyone. The mention of his name filled people with awe. He was "Mr. Success."

He accepted my invitation immediately and asked if we might eat at his club. It was a lunch hour I'll never forget. He asked me about my plans for a business career. He told me that a man can get just about anything he wants if he really wants it—said it's all a matter of drive.

He talked for an hour—fast and strong—sensibly. I got more stimulation out of that lunch hour than I would have gotten from the boys in a year. People saw me go out and come back with the big man—and other big shots in the company saw us at the club. I was no longer just one of the clerks to other people—and more important I was no longer just one of the clerks to myself.

Are you spending the lunch hour with the same people every day—people whose minds you know like a book—people who no longer offer any stimulation to you—people who go over the same old gripes, the same old stories?

I soon found that the lunch hour could be turned into a powerhouse by eating with different people in the company—by having lunch dates with people in other companies. I picked up ideas, important news, inspiration, stimulation. It sharpened the edge of my ambition.

This whole process of channeling your money—your time—your energy—into your goals can be started by asking yourself the one vital question about every dime and dollar you spend. This technique is the greatest of drive-builders. It's the great unifier. It lops away all miscellaneous expenditures, not only of money but of hours, and of personal force. It concentrates your power—channels it where it must go in order to get you the big things you want.

Hobbies or a career

This technique will run you smack into the question of hobbies—it will force you to answer the question of whether you're pursuing a hobby or a career. There's nothing wrong with hobbies if they *are* hobbies—but there's a lot wrong with them when you pursue a hobby *in place of* a career. There's something very wrong with trying to get out of your hobby the big main-goal satisfactions that should come from your work.

The unhappy fisherman

A 40-year-old man had never gotten his career off the ground. His hobby was fishing—large mouth black bass—and what's wrong with that? Nothing's wrong with it—but this man carried with him on his fishing trips the cloud of his unrealized goals. He held a small clerky kind of job that didn't use a tenth of his real powers. He had large financial ambitions that he had never seriously tried to realize. He was using his fishing trips to run away from his thwarted life—but it didn't work at all. He was continuously unhappy.

I suggested to him that he use this technique—that he start asking himself the loaded question every time he spent a nickel or any sum of money. I suggested that he keep the money he saved separately in a little box. (This sounds childish and silly, but it helps to dramatize the whole technique.)

Within a week he had a collection of silver and a dollar bill in the box. But asking himself every time he spent anything, "Will this expenditure further my financial career?" soon made him question not only how he was spending his money—but how he was spending his days, his evenings, his energy. It kept the big question right before him. Was he giving himself to the financial success that he wanted? No, of course he wasn't. He was running away from success. He was hotly pursuing failure.

At long last—and at 40 years of age—he faced the facts of his situation. He saw the unyielding truth—that he would never enjoy fishing—or anything else—till he felt he was a success in his own eyes.

He kept up with the technique. It started to channel all

his activities into success—and the more he channeled them the greater his "drive" became. He went all out on his career—became an unqualified success in his field.

Now he can enjoy his fishing—now he enjoys it as a hobby. He enjoys it as an avocation because he has a real vocation. Now when he casts his plug into the lily pads that old cloud of his unfulfilled self is no longer hanging there above the water. And when the bass hits his plug his pleasure is complete. He enjoys his hobby because he doesn't need it. It's now a valuable change of pace from his business career. The hobby is now playing second fiddle to his main-line activity and the harmony is good.

And what about your evenings?

How do you spend the time from 8 to 11 each evening? Do you spend it looking at television? We have nothing against television—but it's no way to spend the whole evening long if you want financial success.

A middle-aged man told me he was dissatisfied—that he wasn't getting anywhere—that he wished he could make some real money. I asked him how he spent his evenings. He said he watched television. And he thinks he wants financial success! He doesn't know what the word *want* means. A hungry man who wants food is out looking for it. A man who really wants financial success is doing something about it. He's working on it. This man said, "I want success and money, all right—but I guess I lack drive."

Thousands of people are in this same boat—people who want financial success enough so they'll never be satisfied without it—but who just don't go out and get it—who don't want it enough to invest themselves in it.

Here's where this technique comes in

Start asking yourself the big question about every dime and dollar you spend: "Will this expenditure further my financial success?" This simple technique can change everything. The actual sums that you save right off will be so much money in your "little box"—but this money is just a forerunner—a heart-warming symbol of the material well-being that can start coming your way as this powerful technique takes hold in your life—as it begins to whip your scattered forces into line.

If you lack drive—if your life is scattered, spread weak and thin all over the lot—this technique can quickly draw the loose ends together. It can lead you into a colorful, stimulating, satisfying existence—filled with financial reward—financial reward that brings with it an ever greater freedom of activity—that leads to the liberation of your true talents in action.

Drive drives out the fear of failure

The reason many people fail is simply that they are afraid they are going to. They never seriously go out after the things they want. They don't want to face a test of their ability to get them. This is especially true of people who lack confidence. They feel they can save hurting their own opinion of themselves—and other people's opinion of them—if they never give themselves wholly to anything.

They tell themselves that they're not succeeding because they're not really trying. This perpetual alibi is meant to save the ego from the pain it might suffer in an out-and-out test of ability that resulted in failure. They realize that nothing fails like failure and they fear making themselves less confident, more failure-minded.

But this technique will strengthen your "want power" —it will build up your financial drive—and when you want success badly enough, you'll no longer think in terms of having confidence. You'll be thinking instead of the ways and means you can use to get the things that you want. So in a very real sense this technique helps to solve the problem of confidence, too.

On the next page is a list of hints
for bringing this technique into play.

Hints for Using This Technique

1. Every time you're about to spend anything—ask your-self, "Will this expenditure contribute to my main financial goal?

2. The value of this technique is not only in the money it saves you—but in its capacity to whip a scattered life into line—to build financial drive.

3. Keep the money you save in a little box. This will dramatize the value of the technique.

4. Each time you ask yourself the big question try to clearly picture your goal on the "screen of your mind."

5. This technique forces the channeling of your money—your time—your energy—your thoughts—into your main goal.

6. It makes you invest in your self—the best investment in the world.

7. Remember that many of a person's expenditures are neutral—for run-of-the-mill stuff that everyone must buy—but make it a habit to ask this question of all expenditures. It keeps the big question continuously before you.

On the next page are a few pointed questions.

A Few Questions to Ask Yourself

1. Do I spend my evenings aimlessly—looking at television—reading the newspaper—in idle talk?

2. Is at least half of all my reading related to my main goal?

3. Do I invest at least two lunch hours a week in my success?

4. Do I at least once a day mentally picture my goal—not as a daydream—but as a goal?

5. Is my hobby a hobby—or is it my main interest?

6. Do I use my money wisely—to serve my main goals?

7. Am I resisting my present job—or using it as a stepping stone in my career?

8. Am I more interested in spending money for prestige than I am in investing it to increase my power and capacity?

If you want to accumulate some money, your answers to the above questions will give you a pretty good idea how much you need the technique explained in this chapter.

Specimen filled-in form. (Showing how a 40-year-old man made out with his first seven days of using this technique. Each time he was about to spend anything he asked himself, "Will this expenditure further me in reaching my financial goal?")

Did I use the technique today?

	Yes	No	Amt. Saved	Remarks
1st day	√		$1.00	Passed up a cocktail on the way home from work. Felt an immediate lift.
2nd day	√		.60	Didn't buy a high-brow magazine to read on train. Studied portion of newspaper dealing with job.
3rd day	√		$3.00	Decided against a tankful of gas for ride in country —spent the Sat. PM in household chores.
4th day	√		.25	Was going to buy a soda which I didn't need or really want. Skipped it.
5th day	√		Nothing	All expenses today were neutral. (Many each day were neutral but asked myself the question just the same.)
6th day	√		.20	Skipped the coffee wagon.
7th day	√		$10.00	My wife and I were going to have dinner out. I asked her if we might better put the money toward a new coat for her. She agreed.

The money saved ($15.05) he placed in a little box—but the big thing he noticed was how this technique had gotten him thinking again about his old financial goals—how it firmed up his jaw about doing something about them.

It forced him to face the big unsettled question. It was his first progress toward building "financial drive."

Form for your use.

(This is your personal work sheet—for a seven-day record of your experience with this technique.)

Did I use the technique today?

	Yes	No	Amt. Saved	Remarks
1st day				....
				....
2nd day				....
				....
3rd day				....
				....
4th day				....
				....
5th day				....
				....
6th day				....
				....
7th day				....
				....

Many expenses each day will be neutral—things like cost of getting to work, buying a paper, buying groceries. But ask yourself the question anyway. The big thing is to keep it before you.

To insure
your financial success

The purpose of this action is to get you working with the most powerful success law known to man.

Here's the technique:

In all transactions make it your chief concern that the person on the other side of the deal gets full value.

This can fill you at once with emotional power—change everything for you virtually overnight. It's the surest road to financial success—the most direct road to a deeply satisfying existence.

Make it your business to give full value—stop worrying about getting everything that's coming to you. Your first job is to see that you give value.

Do this and you won't have to worry about getting.

This is no soft-headed sentimental claptrap. It's a law of steel. There's power in it—psychological power that fills you at once with the expectation of good things to come— and "practical" power that's inherent in the very nature of "giving value"—the most reasonable of all laws: Take care of the other people's interests and they'll take care of yours.

A little ice cream store hits the jackpot

Some years ago in a small town on Long Island there was only one ice cream store and that store never seemed to do very well. There was never enough business around to keep things going.

Then a couple of young fellows came along and took the store over. They followed only one rule—to give full value—and not only full value—but running over. They made their own ice cream and put into it the best ingredients they could buy (it was delicious)—and they made their own chocolates—followed the same formula (they were tops).

More exceptional still were the portions they gave. When you bought a quart of ice cream they'd fill the container so high that the flaps at the top of the box couldn't begin to cover it. When they served you an ice cream soda you got a giant glass filled with a double portion of everything good that should go into a soda. When you bought a pound of chocolates there was no weighing things to a fraction of an ounce. The pointer on the scale would always swing freely over the mark and stay there.

Older people smiled in their superior wisdom and said

it couldn't last. They observed that "under new management" always brought forth a short burst of steam—that "a new broom sweeps clean"—that the boys would have their rude awakening when the economic law caught up with them. This generosity was all very nice, but would they be able to stay in business?

They stayed in business. They throve. This formula worked and it worked with a vengeance. People came from far and wide to get their good ice cream—their delicious candy. But it was the king-sized portions that did the trick—their policy of giving generous overflowing measure. These boys were doing a thriving business when business everywhere else was in the doldrums. Their business philosophy was simply this: to give in everything much more than you were expected or required to give.

The young fellow who was going to get $10,000 a year or quit

I once worked for a company that hired a young fellow —fresh out of college—to learn the business. The first week he was with the company he told his department head that if he wasn't making $10,000 a year in two years he would quit. This was a bit novel if nothing else. Nobody had told us off so quickly before.

Now there's nothing wrong with setting your sights high. There's nothing wrong with wanting to work your way up to $10,000 a year in two years. But I watched this fellow work and I shook my head. His greatest fear seemed to be that he might give the company more than $60 worth of work a week—which is what they paid him. Why should he give them more? $60 a week is what they were paying him and that's what he'd give them in return. If they wanted more from him let them give him a raise. Someone suggested to him that maybe he ought first to show that he was worth more to the company than he was getting—and then he'd be more apt to get it.

The fellow's attitude undid him—and fast. He wasn't worth $60 a week to the company—or anywhere near it. And more important, he knew it. He knew that he was shortchanging his employer. And—cynic though he thought he was—he felt uneasy about it deep inside. This feeling that he was in the wrong caused him to think negatively about his job and his prospects in it. He was fired long before his "$10,000 a year in two years" had a chance to come true—but it never had a chance to come true. He never gave it a chance. He was bucking a universal law—a law so adamant he might just as well have bucked his head against a stone wall—a law which says that if you want to prosper you must give value.

But this law works both ways

I've known scores of men and women with big jobs. All of them had one thing in common. They gave full measure to the people they worked for as they made their way up to these big jobs. They were concerned that things be handled right. They assumed responsibility. They gave their time, their energy, their brains, their enthusiasm to the boss.

Here's a good example

A few years before the fellow who was "going to make $10,000 a year in two years" came with the company, they hired another and very different kind of young man in a similar job. He really gave himself to his little job, went all-out on it. He was the kind of person who believes in giving value. Right from the start he was worth a lot more to the company than they were paying him. He got raise after raise. When quitting time came and the whole place would clear out, he'd still be there at his desk working an extra hour or two whenever it was necessary. Whenever anything needed to be done he was right there to see that it was taken care of.

I watched this man's meteoric rise to one of the four highest jobs in the company—and it's a big company. The management saw at once that he was one of them, that he had their interests at heart as though they were his own—and in reality they were his own.

A sound foundation for positive thinking

Most important of all is what this "giving value" does for your own frame of mind. It fills you with hope in the future. It makes you feel that you have something good coming to you. It gives you a sound foundation for positive thinking—and this is the first essential for the enjoyment of living and for the achievement of material success.

This formula turned the tide for me

Some 20 years ago I was asked by a civic organization to conduct a men's forum that met once a week to discuss the personal problems of living. The organization badly needed a leader—and they assured me that I was the man for the job. Should I take the job? Things were tough with me at the time. I was doing free lance work and writing small bits here and there. The question I had to face was whether I should take on this public service which paid nothing or spend all my energies trying to bring in some additional money. I had heard, of course, about this principle of giving value since the time I was a child—but I had never gone all out on it—had never consciously made it a central formula for living. Here was a chance to try it. I'd get nothing for my labors. Should I take on the free job? Should I start giving?

I decided to take the free job. It meant a lot of time and work but I soon found that the people who asked me to take on this work seemed to know better than I where my special abilities lay. The work was a huge success. I loved it. I discovered that I had the capacity to get other people stirred up, enthusiastic, excited. It regained for me a quickened confidence in my own abilities. It did for me the thing I needed most of all to have done at the time. It primed the pump and got me going again. The thing we need most is to enter into action that will open up our powers, that will release us. The big point is that these activities we enter into in order to give are the greatest pump-primers in the world. They get the water of life flowing through us again.

It is interesting to note that the job I was afraid I couldn't afford to take proved to be the turning point. It set free the power of this mighty principle within me. It led me into a many-sided prosperity that I have enjoyed ever since.

The insurance man who refused to write a $10,000 policy

This insurance man believed in giving value, in looking first to his clients' interests. He believed in it so thoroughly that it was his everyday method of operation. He believed that it was his duty to look out for his people. He believed that if he did this wholeheartedly his commissions would look out for themselves.

One day he got a phone call from a man he had never met. He told the insurance man that a mutual friend had spoken very highly of him—said he was a good man to know. The caller said he wanted to take out a $10,000 straight life policy.

The insurance man thanked him for calling—but told him he wouldn't want to sell him anything until he had fully considered his problem. The man was amazed.

He said, "You're the first insurance man I've run into who wasn't anxious to write insurance. I call you up and tell you I want a $10,000 policy and you won't sell it to me till you've talked with me. What goes on?"

The insurance man told him that it wouldn't be fair to sell him something that might not meet his needs. He said it was his job not only to sell insurance but to see to it that his people got the kind of insurance they needed. He asked for an appointment.

He met the man, a young fellow who was having a hard struggle to get by, who was worried about providing for his wife and family. The insurance man worked out the problem for him, wrote him a policy, term insurance, plus some other arrangement. It gave the young man's family a lot more protection than they would have had with the policy the man had called to buy. Furthermore, it saved him some money in the bargain. The man was grateful. From that day on he looked upon the salesman as "my insurance man." He told everyone what a fine person he is.

This insurance man is writing more insurance in a month

than most men write in a year. He has only one rule and he means it: How can I give more value to the people I serve?

It works everywhere

This is not something that works just once in a while, that works in one place and not in another. It works for anyone who tries it if the person who tries it is really sincere, if the business that tries it really means it. But most of us are so slow to learn this lesson. We're trapped by the fallacy that the way to prosper is to insist on getting everything that's coming to us. We simply don't believe that this law works, no matter how often we see it demonstrated to us.

Each Friday night my wife and I see this law at work as we drive up to our farm a couple of hours out of New York City. There are dozens of eating places along the road and we have tried them all. Most of them are disappointing—a mediocre meal, mediocre cooking, mediocre portions, mediocre service. And they charge a good price, to boot.

The volume of business these places do shows that something is wrong somewhere. You find a dozen people having dinner in a restaurant that accommodates a hundred. We have, though, found one place that gives an excellent meal at a reasonable price, and here you see the law magnificently at work. The place is busy with a happy dinner crowd from five in the afternoon till eleven at night. The owner is giving value. He's not just "running a restaurant" —*he's giving people their dinner*. He's doing a happy, active, thriving business because he is serving the kind of meal he himself would like to have.

When business serves it will prosper

We know in our hearts that business must serve and that it will prosper as it serves. You probably know businesses that are prospering and don't give a tinker's dam about serving. I know such businesses, too. But I have noticed that people who run these businesses that care only for profits, that don't give a hoot about the people they serve, are for the most part scared to death. They must forever maintain their volume of business through high-pressure advertising and selling methods. They must forever run their businesses with an anxious intensity that spoils things for themselves and for everyone who works for them. Those who serve their public well, who give full value, not only prosper materially but can enjoy the luxury of a quiet heart.

A top example of this law at work

My wife and I were driving home after several days on the road. We had been getting indifferent food on the way and we were looking for a good place to eat as we drove down from Cooperstown, New York (Baseball Hall of Fame, Farmers Museum, etc.), toward the city of Oneonta, New York.

As we approached Oneonta we passed a sign at the side of the road that suggested we eat at the Health Bar Restaurant in Bresee's Department Store in Oneonta. After the food we had been eating along the road the idea of a Health Bar Restaurant sounded pretty good to us, and as it was getting near lunch time we decided to eat there.

We got into Oneonta at 11:25, spotted the department

store we were looking for, parked a block or so beyond it and walked back to Bresee's. As we were walking back we wondered if the Health Bar Restaurant would be open this early, if they would be ready to serve lunch a half-hour before noon. We expected to find an eating place with a dozen stools and a counter. We were in for a surprise. The Health Bar accommodates about a hundred people. It was filled nearly to capacity at 11:30 in the morning!

My wife and I managed to find two places together. We sat down and looked around us. Then we looked questioningly at each other, wondering what we had stumbled upon. You could sense at once that this was no ordinary eating place. The place had that aura, that atmosphere, of an establishment where people are fed well. There was an indefinable feeling in the air, a feeling suggesting life and good will, a feeling that's found only in such places. In a few minutes, and well before noon, it was filled to capacity.

A crisp-looking waitress came up to us and asked us what we'd like to have. She smiled, not the usual mechanical skin-deep smile, but the smile of a person who is pleased with her job and wants to please you. We ordered fresh fruit salads, which she courteously explained would take a few minutes and while we were waiting we looked around us. I noticed that a number of people near us were having some kind of chicken pie and it looked so good I wondered if I should have ordered that. Several people were having sandwiches. They were freshly made, packed full with goodness, generous in size. The thought crossed my mind that the person who made them up wasn't just making sandwiches but was preparing someone's lunch.

But it was the pies that caught my eye. They were twice

as thick (or maybe I should say high) as ordinary pies—and I have never seen such mouth-watering masterpieces. The cuts were double size and doubly delicious. Our fruit salads were fresh and crisp and large. The coffee was superb. Everything was as clean as a whistle and to top everything off the service was prompt and pleasant. I told my wife that this is the kind of place I've often imagined myself running, if I ever ran a restaurant. Once in a blue moon you run into something like this, something in a class by itself. It was a delight.

After having tried their Health Bar Restaurant we were anxious to see what the rest of the Bresee's Department Store would be like, and we went into the store proper to look around. Here was the same healthy vibrant atmosphere. Here was fresh attractive merchandise, tastefully displayed. Here were good-looking salespeople, friendly and helpful.

I walked about looking at this and that. Everyone everywhere was genuinely pleasant in an easy unobtrusive way. I bought a necktie, some Russell Stover candies and a couple of large chocolate bars. My wife had gone off to look the store over on her own. She joined me after she had bought a few things. She knows department stores as only an experienced woman shopper can, and she said the place is tops all around. She added that she wished she had a store like this near home to shop in.

I think I know enough about business to know that something like this doesn't just happen. I know that there must be somebody behind this business, somebody with character and imagination—someone who is fired by something more than the simple wish to make a profit. Here are merchants in the finest tradition, in the finest meaning of that word.

When we reached home my wife dropped the store a note to tell them how much we had enjoyed having lunch at the Health Bar and how much we had enjoyed the hour we spent in the store. Mr. Philip W. Bresee answered to thank us and told us something of the work they have been doing. *The business has grown so that it is now doing over $3,000,000 a year (in 1961)—in a town of only 14,000 population! The Health Bar alone has served as many as 3,000 people in one day!*

This organization is prospering because it gives value and gives to overflowing, and it gives this value pleasantly—which in itself is a very important value, too. This store need never worry about its corporate image. It's success is founded upon the solid foundation of a universal law.

But why won't we learn this lesson?

People in business are so reluctant to learn this lesson. When you tell them that the way to thrive is to give value they tell you that you don't understand their business, that it can't be done, that their rent is high, that help is expensive and inefficient.

When you tell a man who has never gotten his life off the ground to try giving, to start by giving his boss full value and he'll soon find things beginning to open up for him, he'll say:

"But you don't know my boss. He lives off fools who give him too much work for a dollar."

Men like this won't see that this law is bigger than any skinflint boss, that it somehow works its way out no matter what your present boss may be like and that sooner or later a man gets back as he gives.

You have three choices—but you must take one

You can't avoid a decision as to what your attitude toward this law of giving will be. You must choose one of the following three courses of action:

1. You can welch on your side of the bargain—try to do as little as you can. This will give you a debit balance in *your own set of books.* You'll be trying to collect more than you're willing to give and you'll feel uneasy. You'll think you have something unpleasant coming to you. You'll be unhappy and the chances are you'll be broke.

2. You can first see how other people deal with you and then treat them just the same in return. This attitude has two big things wrong with it. It means that other people determine for you what your conduct will be. You follow their lead. They act. You re-act. It leaves you without a true principle of action. The second thing wrong with it is that it doesn't permit you to build up an "inner moral credit balance." You won't be overdrawn, but you won't have any balance either.

3. The third choice is one of making it a principle of action to do everything you can for the person on the other side of the deal, to give full value, to see that the other person gets a good bargain. This choice is explosive with power. It puts a dynamic psychological law on your side. It fills you with a

continuous expectation of good to come. It gives you the forceful backing of the great economic truth: that people will reward you when you seriously and generously look out for their interests.

On the next page are some valuable hints for using this liberating technique.

Hints for Using This Technique

1. Whether you work for someone else or run your own business, give the fellow on the other side of the deal full value.

2. As soon as you're more interested in giving than in getting, you'll become more positive-minded, you'll feel that you have something good coming to you.

3. You can further your skill in giving value by asking yourself, "If things were reversed, what kind of deal would please me?"

4. People will reward you if you look out for their interests. There's a powerful law here—and the law works.

5. But it works both ways. They'll want no part of you if you don't give value. And it works in reverse psychologically, too. You'll feel that you have something bad coming to you.

6. One doesn't have to worry about his "corporate image" if he gives value—or about his personal image either. They'll take care of themselves.

7. Remember that this law will work powerfully with you if you give powerfully. The more you give the more you'll have.

Now we come to some exciting charts
for evaluating yourself on "giving value."

On the next page is a specimen filled-in form.

(As filled in by a young man working in the accounting department of a white-collar organization of 3,000 employees.)

The purpose of these ten questions is to see how you rate on giving value. For each question put a check in one of the three columns.

	Minus	So-So	Plus
1. If a fellow worker asks me a question, do I resent the bother —or am I glad to help?			✓
2. If a situation arises which means working an hour late—am I put out about it or glad to help?		✓	
3. When a problem comes up that calls for some "brain sweat," do I balk or do my best?	✓		
4. Do I worry about being given credit for everything I do?	✓		
5. Am I trying to think up ways to do things better and turning in such suggestions?			✓
6. Do I work steadily through the day—or do I kid around?		✓	
7. Do I try to put myself across with talk—or do I let my performance stand for me?		✓	
8. If a customer phones for information, do I try to treat him as the boss would, or do I just try to get rid of the call?	✓		
9. If the boss hands me back a piece of work and tells me why it won't do, do I sulk or welcome the chance to improve it?		✓	
10. If I'm asked to do something I consider beneath me jobwise, do I get on my high horse or do I gladly do it for the business?	✓		

Any such chart as this has its limitations as a method for accurately grading you on "giving value," but it will give you a quick rough idea of how you rate. This young man has his eye on a top executive job. With only two checks in the plus column it isn't good.

Form for your use. (This is for business people; form for non-business people follows.)

Rate yourself on giving value. After each question put a check in one of the three columns.

	Minus	So-So	Plus
1. If a fellow worker asks me a question, do I resent the bother —or am I glad to help?			
2. If a situation arises which means working an hour late—am I put out about it or glad to help?			
3. When a problem comes up that calls for "brain sweat," do I balk or do my best?			
4. Do I worry about being given credit for everything I do?			
5. Am I trying to think up ways to do things better and turning in such suggestions?			
6. Do I work steadily through the day—or do I kid around?			
7. Do I try to put myself across with talk—or do I let my performance stand for me?			
8. If a customer phones for information, do I try to treat him as the boss would, or do I just try to get rid of the call?			
9. If the boss hands me back a piece of work and tells me why it won't do, do I sulk or welcome the chance to improve it?			
10. If I'm asked to do something I consider beneath me jobwise, do I get on my high horse or do I gladly do it for the business?			

Score yourself now for *last* week. Try giving value for a week *after* you've read this chapter. Note how your score improves.

FOR NON-BUSINESS PEOPLE

(Read this before you rate yourself on "giving value.")

This law of giving value works in all walks of life—not only between employee and employer—not only between businessman and customer. Giving value bears rich fruit in our "contracts"—social, community, family, friends.

One of the greatest personal benefits is the way it drives out fear. When we make it a principle of living to more than fulfill our obligations, we then naturally assume that people are well disposed toward us. We feel that we have something good coming to us. It brings peace of mind and fills us with a continuous expectation of good to come. Every person is a bookkeeper, first and last—keeps his own set of books—debiting himself when he pays less than he should, crediting himself when he pays more than the situation demands.

When we make this principle of "giving value" basic to all our actions we then know that our attitude is right—and this knowledge makes us strong when we must ask something reasonable of others.

Example: If a neighbor's dog is a nuisance and you have to speak to him about it—and if your principle of action is one of generously meeting others more than half way— then you'll handle the matter without fear or anger, with friendly self-assurance. Your own generous attitude makes you assume you'll get co-operation. When your attitude is based on this principle you act in a way that invites it.

This principle has behind it a powerful all-pervasive law and whole-hearted obedience to the spirit of that law brings not only material well being but a host of other warm personal benefits as well, all down the line.

The next page shows how a non-business person, a suburban housewife answered the list of questions to see how she rates in giving value. Read it over and then rate yourself on the form that follows it.

Specimen filled-in form. (As filled in by a non-business person—a suburban housewife.)

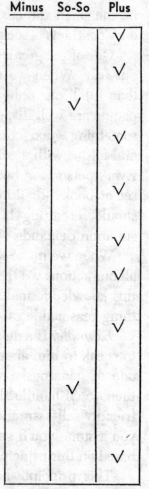

The purpose of this list is to rate yourself in "giving value." For each question put a check in one of the three columns.

	Minus	So-So	Plus
1. Am I generous-minded in my dealings with my neighbors?			√
2. Do I carry my full share of the chore load in the home?			√
3. Do I smile when I greet people who don't smile at me?		√	
4. Do I have a sense of responsibility in the community—or just live there?			√
5. Do I do any "social work" gratis (scouting, making bandages, etc.)?			√
6. Am I courteous to other drivers when I'm at the wheel?			√
7. Am I careful that none of my activities is a nuisance to my neighbors?			√
8. Do I ever make a personal sacrifice to make a charitable contribution?			√
9. Am I willing to meet people more than half way when we disagree, if so doing doesn't involve the sacrifice of principle?		√	
10. Do I send birthday cards to family members outside my immediate household?			√

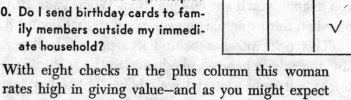

With eight checks in the plus column this woman rates high in giving value—and as you might expect she's a happy individual.

Rating ourselves on any such quality as "giving value" can't be done with mathematical accuracy—but our answers to this list of questions can give us a rough idea of where we stand.

Form for your use.

(This is for non-business people.)

Rate yourself on giving value. After each question put a check in one of the three columns.

	Minus	So-So	Plus
1. Am I generous-minded in my dealings with my neighbors?			
2. Do I carry my full share of the chore load in the home?			
3. Do I smile when I greet people who don't smile at me?			
4. Do I have a sense of responsibility in the community—or just live there?			
5. Do I do any "social work" gratis (scouting, making bandages, etc.)?			
6. Am I courteous to other drivers when I'm at the wheel?			
7. Am I careful that none of my activities is a nuisance to my neighbors?			
8. Do I ever make a personal sacrifice to make a charitable contribution?			
9. Am I willing to meet people more than half way when we disagree, if so doing doesn't involve the sacrifice of principle?			
10. Do I send birthday cards to family members outside my immediate household?			

Score yourself now for *last* week. Try giving value for a week after you've read this chapter. Note how your score improves.

To break through the barrier that limits the size of your thinking

The purpose of this technique is to enable you to break through the ceiling that limits the size of the thoughts you can think—that limits the size of the goals you can set up—that limits the size of the ways and means you can come up with for their realization.

Here's the technique:

Imagine that you're suddenly faced with the necessity of doing things on ten times the scale you're now operating.

I can hear your impatient reply, "Ten times the scale? The man's crazy!"

But that's just the reaction you're supposed to have. It's supposed to shock you. The whole value of this technique is in the jolt it gives. We desperately need something to shock us out of our habitual round of "small-time thinking." This is no place for half measures. When we use half measures, when, for example, we tell ourselves we must do "a little better" nothing is basically changed. We then go on thinking and acting in the same old size-pattern. But when we use this "ten-times technique," and use it right, it wakes us up like a clap of thunder. We stop short, see everything with a fresh eye, reappraise everything we're doing, dramatically change our method of operation.

Thinking big sets imaginative people on fire

When I talked with a friend about this chapter he thought I should leave it out of the book. Here was his objection:

> How many people are interesting in thinking big, or in being big, for that matter? All most people want is to be a bit better off than they are. They want to move up from a Falcon to a Buick, from a $12,000 home in Levittown to a $20,000 ranch house in Huntington, from $8,000 a year to $12,000 a year.

Here was my answer to him:

> This book is being written for people who want to do something special with their lives, for people who believe they have something special inside them to which they must give expression. These people often need a big canvas on which to work. The thing that

holds them back is the artificial limitation that hems in the size of the thoughts they can think. The thing that frustrates them is their inability to encompass mental concepts that are big enough for their potential capacities. Projects of real dimension set the capabilities of such people on fire. Big thinking, when you need it, when it suits your potential, is very fiery stuff.

But we don't think big

A psychologist once told me that the thoughts any person can think are limited by the culture in which he lives. Something akin to this is at work in our lives limiting the size of the thoughts we can think.

It is said that people who have never seen a mountain can't picture one. But that's not precisely what keeps us from thinking big. Figuratively speaking, we *have* seen a mountain. We have seen and heard of other people who have done great things. The trouble is we can't think of *ourselves* as doing things of real dimension. We can't picture a *mountain of our own.*

There are many factors that hold down the size of the thoughts a person can think:

The portion of society from which he comes— his estimate of his own powers—what others expect of him—what he expects of himself—how deserving he feels—the amount of needling he gets from his wife—the scale on which he is now operating. All these tend to set the dimension in which he thinks. He gets thinking in a certain size-pattern, and habit and inertia do the rest.

$12,000 or $60,000 a year

Why, for example, does a man think he should try to make $12,000 a year? Because for some reason or other $12,000 seems right and proper to him. Why shouldn't the same man aim at $60,000 a year? Because it doesn't fit what he thinks should be his picture of himself.

Here's an actual situation that illustrates how the size of our thinking keeps us from taking success-making action even when the door is thrown wide open to us. Some years ago a man was making $3,600 a year—which he thought was pretty good; but his goal was to make $5,000 a year— the magic figure that somehow spelled financial success to him. One day he heard of a good job being open in his line of work. It paid $10,000 a year. He felt he should take action on this opportunity, but something was holding him back. He spoke to his father about it. His father advised him as follows:

"If the company is as good as your present company and you think you can handle the job, then go ahead and get it."

The young man began to make excuses but they didn't ring true to his father, who told him:

"I think $10,000 a year seems so big to you it scares the daylights out of you."

His father was right. He never went after that job. The young fellow couldn't think of himself "as if" he were a $10,000 man.

Here's where the technique comes in

We can jolt ourselves out of the prison that limits the size of our thinking by using this "ten-times technique."

We can break free from the "squirrel cage" in which our little aims run round and round, get out into the fresh air, dramatically increase the size of the projects we are able to embrace, discover as if by magic electric new means for the realization of these bigger goals. Just use this technique. Tell yourself that you must operate on ten times the scale you're now operating, or that you must do something ten times as well as you're now doing it. This "as if" concept will smash through the ceiling that limits the size of your thinking.

> Sometimes this process is forced on us from the outside and then we don't have to imagine it, as in the exciting example that follows.

The young man who was "shocked" by his company president

One morning when John, a young $10,000 corporate executive, arrived at his office, his secretary told him, "Mr. Wells would like to see you in his office at ten this morning."

Mr. Wells was the president of the company, and he *never* sent for minor executives. John wondered what was up. He felt uneasy. He assumed that something must be wrong. He hoped he was in for just a bawling out but thought maybe he was going to be fired as part of the company's austerity program. ("That would be austerity for me, all right," he observed wryly.)

In the hour he had before he was due in the president's office he reassured himself, or tried to. He had done a pretty good job with his department. Profits had gone up about ten percent each year for the two years he had been running the department. He hadn't set the world on fire but he had shown that he was no slouch. He felt better after having given himself this line of reassurance—and with his department's latest profit and loss statement in his hand he headed "upstairs."

As soon as he came into the president's office the big boss said to him,

"I think you have some very good stuff in you, John, but your department is showing a profit of only $100,000 a year."

So that was it. He felt better. He could vindicate himself here.

"Yes, Mr. Wells, but that's up about ten percent from last year, isn't it?"

Mr. Wells didn't answer. He just paused for a few seconds as though he were setting the stage for something—and then came the haymaker.

"In the next two years I want you to try to step up profits in your department to a million dollars a year."

John thought perhaps that he had heard the big boss wrong. He swallowed hard.

"Did you say a million, sir?"

"Yes, a million."

"But that's ten times what I'm now doing. You're not joking with me sir?" he asked hopefully.

"No, I'm certainly not joking. I want you to try it—and with the same people you now have. When you show a million in profits your salary will be increased to $25,000 a year."

John was silent for a moment, trying to pull himself together, trying to get his bearings.

"I'll do what I can, Mr. Wells. I hope you don't mind

my saying so but I'm flabbergasted. This comes as a great surprise to me. It's given me a terrific jolt."

Mr. Wells permitted himself a little inward smile. He had gotten just the response he was after. He knew that John was an able person using a fraction of his real potential. He knew that the thing he and nearly everyone else needs is just such "a terrific jolt"—something strong enough to free their thinking from the little cage in which it is trapped.

John had gotten a jolt, all right—but it was a happy jolt. He was all agog at the possibility of making $25,000 a year (when you're making $10,000 a year $25,000 seems like paradise)—and he wanted very much to please Mr. Wells, whom he liked and admired. Two powerful emotions had entered the picture to break things wide open: the chance for financial gain—and the desire for approval. Madame de Staël says it's the emotions that make us think—and it's the emotions that make us think big.

John breaks through his ceiling

By the time John got back to his desk he was a new man moving in a new world. For the first time in his life he felt that he was really alive. For the first time he felt an exhilarating flow of energy that seemed to carry him along and make everything easy. He reappraised everything he was doing, gave everything an electric going over. He'd have to find some radically new way to operate, totally different from his present method. He had been shocked out of his usual way of life. He started to act big—to match the great new vision that Mr. Wells' explosive action had planted in his mind.

His department made its money selling $5 books by mail. He'd keep this "flywheel" going of course and try to rev it up—but his mind began to race over new territory. Under the powerful stimulus of his new vision he jotted down a dozen ideas that "thinking big" had set blazing in his mind.

He'd now sell 1,000 to 10,000 copies of a book at a clip to larger corporations. He'd branch out from his book business and add "art prints" to his line. He'd bring out a $300 "Culture Library." He'd climb aboard the home-study-course-boom (one of the fastest growing businesses in America). His imagination was flashing off ideas, his judgment had a new razor-like edge.

But the biggest change of all in John was his sudden transformation from executive to leader. His new fire spread rapidly to everyone around him. He now had something to fight for, something he wanted intensely, and this wanting something intensely is the essence of leadership—the thing that enables one person to set others on fire. Business is begging for this quality today—home life needs it—it's the heart of politics, all organization work—and the quickest way to achieve this quality is to break through to THINKING BIG.

In a matter of hours John and his department were functioning at a whole new tempo. One of the most interesting points of this awakening was the way he used on his own advertising copywriters the technique Mr. Wells had used on him. He told them no longer to try for quota—but to write "as if" they had to make *ten times quota!* They smiled when they heard it—but the stepped-up copy some of them started to turn out showed the dynamic power in this ten-times technique.

This works on engineers, too

An engineer had this same thing pulled on him in a slightly different way. His company was marketing a piece of equipment that retails for $10 and is used in almost every building in the country. The market is enormous—but the competition is tough.

One day the boss asked him to try to figure out some way that would enable them to sell the $10 product for $1. The engineer gave the boss a quick look to see if he had been drinking. He looked sober enough even though he didn't sound it. The engineer protested indignantly, "But you simply can't sell anything like that for a dollar."

"Right. You can't. But I didn't say it would have to be 'anything like that.' My guess is that it will have to be something very unlike our present product."

The engineer had to stand way back from the operation and try to see the whole thing in new perspective. His whole approach changed. He started thinking all over again from the ground up. Within three weeks he came through with a whole new idea—based on a totally different principle—something so different, so simple, they could market it for $5 at a good profit and practically take over the field.

This technique of "as-if-ten-times-the-size"—or in this case, "as-if-one-tenth-the-cost"—magically breaks us free from the cage of habits in which our thoughts go round and round. We try too often to modify things, to improve them—which is all right as far as it goes—but what we sometimes need is to blast ourselves into a whole new approach—and this "as-if-ten-times" technique is the very thing that can do it.

And it increases your energies and capacities

This technique not only blasts us into *new thinking*, but, equally important, it enormously increases our capacities, our energies. Here is one of the greatest of all psychological miracles: When we force ourselves into big thinking, when we envision new plans and king-sized goals, the inner self automatically tries to "up your output" to supply "what it takes" to put across these big new plans. It automatically tries to supply the increased capacity to match your daring new vision.

Psychologists have been telling us for years how this mechanism works on the physical level. They have given us a very simple illustration of this mechanism in action— something which everyone has experienced. Here it is:

> When you reach out to lift something that you think is going to be heavy and it turns out to be light, the thing goes shooting up into the air.

Why? Because you thought you had to lift something heavy and thus you were ready to lift something heavy. *We automatically* try to put forth the degree of strength we think a task requires.

For example: Suppose you're going to lift a five-gallon can of gasoline. You know what it weighs—you've lifted them before. (Actually it's 35 pounds.) Without thinking about it your mind *thinks* 35 pounds. It dials 35 pounds to your muscles and nerves. We never think of this mechanism unless we get fooled by the can being empty. Then it weighs less than a tenth as much—and the three-pound empty can goes sailing up over our heads with a 35-pound tug.

No matter what we think a task requires we automatically try to respond with the force necessary to take care of it. When we break through to big new thinking—when we entertain big new goals—envision things in a whole new dimension—and hold that vision before us, our energies and capacities are automatically stepped up to meet the increased demand.

Anyone can use this "as-if-ten-times technique" anywhere

You can use this technique anywhere to multiply your power. You can use it in your business, you can use it in charity work, in social goings-on, in church work, and you can use it at home. It takes no special equipment. You can turn it on in a matter of minutes. Just imagine that you're faced with the necessity of making one of your operations ten times as big—or ten times as successful—or ten times as good as it is. This "as if" technique can bring a whole new dimension into any area of your life.

For example, I used this technique in working on this book

When I began to write this book I was naturally interested in how large a sale it would have. I knew from experience that books of this kind usually sell around 10,000 copies and I had been thinking in terms of 10,000 copies. But why shouldn't I use this thinking big technique on the book? Why shouldn't I think in terms of 100,000 copies instead of 10,000 copies? Why not multiply the operation by ten?

I imagined I was under the necessity of writing not just a better book than I had planned—but something *ten times as good*. One that would warrant a sale of 100,000 copies. I reminded myself I was writing this book to do people some good, and that it would be better to do good to 100,000 people than to 10,000. I recalled how such a book would have helped me when I was a young man—and I wanted to give my son and young people like him the advantage of my experiences.

I spent an evening getting myself into thinking big about the book—drumming up the emotions that would incite me to break through to big thinking about it. Suddenly the whole thing came through with a roar, breaking me free from the too-small pattern in which my thinking about the book had been trapped.

I had known from the start that my general idea for the book was good. The idea was this: to explain a dozen principles that step up a person's effectiveness, things that I know from experience work. This shaped up nicely and I was satisfied with it—but now that I was using this "ten-times-technique" my stance toward the whole project changed. I decided that this wasn't going to be "just another book" but something very special. Under the electric charge of this "as if" technique the pulse beat of the whole project stepped up.

A dozen ideas for making the book a better book came to me with rapid-fire speed. Now the book would not only deal with specific actions but would feature those actions in a striking new way. To begin with I'd set the book up not as Chapter 1, Chapter 2, and so on—but as Action 1, Action 2, etc.

Each chapter (Action) would start right off with a one-sentence statement of the purpose of the action to be taken—and be followed by a one-sentence description of the action itself. My "thinking big" about the book gave the whole project new pace and power and improved it in a dozen ways.

I decided to supply at the end of each Action the forms the reader needs to make the taking of these actions virtually automatic. I called these vital pages at the end of each "chapter" the "business-end of the chapter." They became the feature of the book.

Thanks to this "as if" technique I had used on myself, I came up with a book that was ten times as valuable to anyone who used it. When the editor read the manuscript he told me it was one of the most exciting self-help books he had ever seen.

Why this technique is such a bombshell

This technique is a terrific bombshell because it brings into play the great psychological principle of "as if." In this case we get the mind to respond "as if" it faced an ultimatum, as if it faced an "or else"—either you step things up to ten times the scale, or do something ten times as well, or else.

You may say this is nothing but a trick, that all we are doing is kidding the mind into believing it must do something that it really need not do. Of course it's a trick—but when used rightly it works. We must remember that the forces which limit the size of our thinking are in a sense artificial, too. They are not necessarily inherent in our make-ups, or in our environment. We can overcome these "artificial" limitations with a contrived technique of our own.

Are you a trail blazer?

The great advantage of this technique is that it permits you to break out of "squirrel cage" thinking, frees you to think fresh new thoughts, take dramatic new approaches. This is a quality that makes a person lead, instead of follow. My father understood men, and he knew how rare originality is; he knew how quick people are to imitate any spark of originality in others. One of his favorite sayings was "It's easy enough to do a thing after somebody else has done it." But the big prizes in life—and more important—the creative satisfactions, go to the person who can initiate, who can lead the way into fresh thinking, and this technique is invaluable for enabling you to do just that.

Warning

This is strong medicine. It will jolt you into a dynamic new life, will lead you into superlative achievements—but there are a couple of things you'd better keep in mind:

1. Don't count on this technique alone to carry the whole load. Don't just sit around thinking big. Using this technique doesn't mean that you can neglect the solid techniques in the other chapters. For example, you must use this electric technique *on top of* the actions outlined for starting off from your "here and now"—for doing your best with things as they are.

2. And you must not junk your current operations. Remember that whatever we are doing is carrying us. Our current activities are the flywheel of our existence. We must keep things going. If we are selling

shoelaces for a living we must continue to sell shoe-laces while we are moving over into thinking big and acting big.

The false objection to bigness

There is a cult today against bigness of any kind. Some of this is a pose, a kind of vanity in reverse, pure pretension, and pure horse feathers. But some of it is real. Bigness *in itself* is not a virtue. To make a thing bigger is not to make it better.

There is an optimum size for everything, whether it be vegetables, a house, or a business operation. To go beyond that size is to run into a diminishing return in satisfaction, in efficiency, or in profit, or in all three. But the optimum size is usually much larger than we in our "squirrel cage" thinking are able to envision—and very often it is not simply a question of the optimum size for a given project—but of changing and adding to the operation, making it a different project where the optimum size is many times larger.

Forms for the dynamic application of this technique
are supplied in the pages that follow.

Hints for Using the "As If"
Technique for Big Thinking

1. Imagine that you're faced with making one of your operations ten times as successful, or ten times its current size, or with becoming ten times as good at something.

2. The purpose of this technique is to enable you to break free from habitual "squirrel cage" thinking—to enable you to take a fresh look at what you're doing—to take a dynamic new approach.

3. Most of our thinking is modification and improvement of what you're doing—which is O.K.—but we often need radical new thinking—a whole new approach.

4. This technique not only breaks you free for big new thinking—but by enabling you to envision big new goals —your capacity and energy are thus increased.

5. Don't go off the deep end and just sit around thinking big. This technique is to be used on top of our regular "flywheel" activities—and along with the rest of the techniques in this book.

6. You can use it anywhere. A housewife can use it to become ten times as good a cook. A real estate man can use it to skyrocket his income from $5,000 to $50,000 dollars a year—an executive can use it to make his judgment virtually infallible.

7. Remember that the optimum size of a project is often much larger than we think it is—whether its our salary— or our business—or any project whatever.

*On the next page is the specimen form
as filled in by a real estate man who
wanted ten times the income he was making.*

Specimen form for getting into big thinking. (As used by a small-time real estate broker—running a little office—with two salesmen working for him—and netting around $5,000 a year.)

My "As If" for Breaking Into Big Thinking

I'm going to imagine I'm faced with the necessity of making $50,000 a year—and act accordingly.

(This man spent an hour getting this "as if" across to himself, his first big step. Just thinking of himself as a $50,000-a-year man changed his whole stance toward himself and his business. His life lit up like a neon sign when he put this "as if" across.)

Here are some of the dramatic new actions I'm going to take:

1. To call attention to my business I'll paint my little building electric yellow and jet black. This will look pretty startling—but it will be the "eye-center" of town.

2. To call attention to myself I'll volunteer to be the speaker at the next meeting of the businessman's luncheon club. I'll give a talk on how to wake up your business and how I'm waking up mine.

3. I've heard of an incentive system for salesmen worked out by a California broker that's sending profits through the roof. It's so hot for salesmen it's set the office on fire. I'll adopt it.

4. I'll have to find some big new deals in business propery—and I'll have to know something about the tax angles involved. I'll bone up on Federal tax angles.

5. I'll make my office an "investment center"—show people how they can get three times the income from real estate as from other investments.

6. I'll get out a little newspaper dramatizing the properties I have for sale.

7. I'll get myself and my men to work up "swapping deals"—this is big stuff now. Instead of one sale you get two, three or more at a clip.

8. I'll go in for "looking like a success"—make a point of being well groomed and well dressed.

This ten-times technique is terrific for revving up your life, breaking it wide open. Try it in some area. See how big thinking transforms your life.

My "As If" for Breaking Into Big Thinking

Date ....

I'm going to break through the ceiling that limits the size of my thinking. To achieve this I'm going to imagine that I must multiply by ten ....
(Fill in your goal on this line.)

Here are some of the actions I'm going to take to achieve it:

1. ....
2. ....
3. ....
4. ....
5. ....
6. ....
7. ....
8. ....

You can use this technique to skyrocket your income —to become ten times as good at your job—to become a savant in any field—to become a terrific cook—to greatly improve your appearance—to achieve power and prestige.

It doesn't matter what the field. This "as if" works. Once you put the "as if" over—once you break through to big thinking—things begin to happen inside you.

You'll fill in the above spaces with exciting new ideas for achieving your bigger vision. You'll find yourself teeming with new energy to achieve your bigger dreams.

Now let's turn to Part V—the most exciting of all: How to launch out on a victorious new life—starting right where we are.

PART V

HOW TO LAUNCH OUT
FROM YOUR CURRENT SET-UP

The three actions in this section are the rockets for launching your great new victorious life. Their powerful thrust will lift you out of your current set-up with breath-taking speed. Here they are—

Action I

This action enables you to single out the few main points that matter in your set-up and concentrate heavily on them. This brings dynamic new power into every area of your life—from the very first minute you use it.

Action 2

This action spotlights an exciting array of new opportunities, opportunities to better yourself in every way—to step up your efficiency enormously—to achieve fast progress in your job—to find new money-making situations by the score.

Action 3

This is the one action with which all progress must start. Without this realistic action you're tied hand and foot. It launches you out from things *just as they are today*—starts you off from your "here and now" (the only place you can possibly start) into an exciting, successful, satisfying existence.

If you can't start from your "here and now" you never start. Here are the three "miracle actions" to launch you off with tremendous speed from the set-up you're in today.

To increase
your effectiveness immediately

The purpose of this action is to get you to concentrate on the few things that matter and literally multiply your capacity.

Here's the technique:

Ask yourself this question about everything you're doing: "What is the heart of this problem? this project? this operation? What one, two, or three points are the essence of the matter?"

This simple technique enables you to separate the essentials from the nonessentials. Use it for a week and you'll find a dynamic new force entering into every area of your existence. It makes you stop wasting your strength on the small-time aspects of your activities, lets you put your energies into the areas that count. Here is the one quality that makes all the difference in people. Here is what makes one person a pygmy and another a giant. You must develop in yourself the habit of sizing up every situation, looking for the few main points on which success in any matter hangs.

The boss who got lost with a slide rule

A fuss-budgetty older man was made head of a department, a department that brought in millions of dollars a year. This department was suddenly presented with an opportunity where huge profits could be made by some very fast, timely action. Instead of dropping everything and riding herd on this opportunity, the old fuss-budget got himself enmeshed in the inconsequential details of a new floor plan for his department. He spent a couple of days deciding where the typewriters and wastebaskets should be placed and just how much space each desk should have. He solved his floor plan and missed his big opportunity.

This example may seem like an exaggeration but it actually happened—and something akin to this is so common that the tendency to place the emphasis in the wrong place might properly be called *THE BIG MISTAKE*. The greatest difference in people is not in brains (and goodness knows this varies widely enough) but in the ability to see what really matters. This is what makes one person electric in everything he touches, keeps another person a lightweight. You may say this is nothing but common sense, but it's common sense in letters a foot high and is one of the most uncommon things in the world.

You can use this technique for everything

This technique can be applied to any situation: your home life, your social life, your job projects and goals. It can even be used for choosing a wife. One man found in this way that there were only three things that mattered (to him) in choosing a wife: that she be healthy, that she be a realist, that she have a happy temperament. (Some of us might conceivably come up with a few other attributes which we consider desirable in a wife.)

The whole point of this exercise is to make you adept in spotting the big essentials. If you have any pretensions to leadership or top-level success, or if you simply want to be reasonably effective in handling things, this ability is a Must.

Efficiency experts

Efficiency experts give us many pointed examples of the value of seeing the few things that matter, or the unhappy result in not seeing them. These experts (now called Management Consultants) vary a great deal. Some of them are good for a short laugh. Some of them are so good they can virtually make a company.

Years ago when efficiency experts were a new thing, my father hired one of them to step up profits in his factory. The factory made, among other things, something called a "Perfecto Bedpan," (or some such thing) which appeared on invoices as "Perf. Bedpan." One day the efficiency expert came to my father with an invoice in his hand and asked him, "How about these perforated bedpans?"

My father exploded. "What are you talking about? Perforated Bedpans!"

For years after that whenever anyone mentioned efficiency experts my father would snarl "Perforated Bedpans!"

But that wasn't the worst shortcoming of some of these early experts. They couldn't see the woods for the trees. They had no sense of the big things that matter. My father wanted help on the big aspects of profits, and they showed him where to place his filing cabinets! This brought forth a scathing blast of sarcasm whenever anyone asked him if efficiency experts were any good.

"Are they any good? They're terrific at figuring out where your filing cabinets should stand. Any man who's hounded by that problem should call them in at once."

But nowadays the good ones have developed to a high degree the ability to see the few things that matter. One consultant showed a company how to zoom profits by placing its ablest men in a half dozen big crucial profit spots throughout the company.

Success is where you make it—and this technique makes it everywhere

A man was promoted to Scout Executive in a big suburban county and right from the start he was so phenomenally successful that everyone wanted to know how he had done it.

He was an exponent of the "few things that matter." He saw at once that the success of scouting in his territory would depend on his ability to get enough good men to volunteer as Scoutmasters. This was the problem, the number one problem, the point on which everything hung. He gave it everything, focused all his energies on it. He got 30 good men to volunteer their services, and scouting boomed in the county.

A company president makes it his rule of action and becomes great

One of the most vital company presidents in America today uses this technique of "the few things that matter" as his central method of operation. He knows that the success of his company rests on these four things:

1. Constantly getting good new products and constantly improving the old ones.

2. Marketing these products dynamically.

3. Being tough on keeping costs down.

4. Keeping everyone stirred up and planning ahead.

He hits these four things and he hits them hard. At his job he's just as successful as Napoleon was at his—and for the same reason. He uses exactly the same strategy as Napoleon used. Napoleon would decide at what precise point he must hit the enemy's line and once that decision was made he would hit that spot with everything, relentlessly, till it broke.

This company president won't discuss a minor problem with anyone. He says that people will solve their own minor problems if you don't do it for them and in most cases it won't make any difference whether they solve them or not.

Bill O'Hare—the nearest thing to genius

Bill O'Hare, that highly gifted advertising man, knows the value of the "few things that matter technique." To talk over your problems with Bill is to have them simplified, to see them in the process of being solved. He has the uncanny ability to see the heart of any problem.

Years ago it was my privilege to work with Bill. He knows all about advertising, all about printing. One day a young mail order copywriter went to him for help:

"Mr. O'Hare, do you think I should use Roman or Italic for this line of small type I want to place across the bottom of the order cards?"

Bill O'Hare is the soul of good nature, but he has nothing but contempt for people who make a big problem out of some inconsequential detail. In his beautifully clipped Boston accent he let the young man have it.

"If you're going to worry about things of that size you'll wind up a clerk. You seem to have all the makings of a good clerk so you'll have to be careful. Try to remember that you're writing an advertising letter, that you're selling something. You have only four things to worry about: (1) Is your letter built around a good central idea? (2) Is the idea written up with persuasive power? (3) Does the letter look right for its purpose? (4) Are you sending the letter to the right people?

"These four are your only real problems. Take care of these and forget about the rest. Whether a little line of type should be Roman or Italic is something for a small mind to worry about. If you put your efforts into problems of that size you'll wind up a dazzling mediocrity."

How small can you get—and how large?

Companies are always putting on cost-cutting campaigns, and all that groaning you hear throughout the land is from the middle management executives each time they hear they must come through with a new list of suggestions for cutting costs.

But here is a chance to show your caliber. There are always a lot of suggestions from the lightweights which are not worth a hoot, ways to save $2 a month on paper clips that cost $8 a month to put over.

This technique of "the few things that matter" immediately separates the men from the boys. The men know that if they're going to save worthwhile amounts they'll have to save it where the big money is spent. One executive jotted down a list of all the places in the company where substantial sums are spent. Overtime was one of these. He came up with the suggestion that no one be permitted to work overtime unless the head of the department worked down, too—and that a memo be sent to the president each time anyone worked overtime, explaining what it was all about. It cut overtime throughout the company virtually in two.

Don't worry about oversimplification

People often fear that this technique will lead them to neglect some angle that matters, that they'll miss out on something that's later discovered to have been important. Actually it works the other way. This technique develops within you a sharp sense of the relative importance of things. You soon become adept at separating the wheat from the chaff.

But suppose it should make you miss out on some point that is important? Even then you won't be as badly off as you'd be if you were fussing about every little thing. When you fail to use this technique you run the risk of losing out on everything that's big and central, you miss the very heart of the matter.

The psychology of evasion

We must say a word about those people who purposely worry about little things so that their preoccupation with these little things makes it impossible for them to face up to the real issues of their lives. This is the way we often kid ourselves. When we are all wrapped up in the little side show it excuses us from going into the main tent. But even here this technique will help us. It will show us that we are evading the main issue (if we are), and just this understanding of what we are doing may help us. And it will make the main tent less of a threat if we know that the main tent is all that we have to worry about, that we have only three real problems and not fifteen.

The aristocrats of our day use this technique all the time

The leaders in every walk of life—top executives, social leaders, political leaders—the people in power—the vital few who are enjoying exciting, rewarding, successful lives—virtually live this technique of the few things that matter. Let's profit by their successful experience. Take a leaf out of their book. Develop in yourself this ability to see the few things that matter and you can go anywhere, do anything. Have you ever noticed how amazed everyone is when the head of a company in one field becomes the head of another company in another field, a field that's new to him? People wonder how he's able to do it. The answer lies in this technique. These men know that in any situation there are just a few things to look for—a few points on which success of the enterprise hinges. They have the faculty for quickly seeing what these main points are and concentrating their energies upon them.

The next few pages give you the material you need to put this dynamic technique to work in your life—and remember it works everywhere.

Hints for Using the Technique of "The Few Big Things That Matter"

1. This technique can be used in any situation, for any problem: for helping a child who's having trouble in school, for buying a house, for handling a tough new problem in your job, for getting to feel better physically, for making your wife (or your husband) happier.

2. The first step in the technique is to state the problem briefly. (See form that follows.) Then try to spot the main factors in the situation—the important considerations on which everything hangs.

3. On the next page is a sample filled-in form showing how a husband used this technique to make his wife happier—and the following page is a sample filled-in form of how he used this technique to get himself feeling better.

4. There are of course a score of factors that affect any problem to some extent—but there are usually three or four main points that dominate the matter.

Now let's turn to the next page and an actual example of this technique in action.

Specimen form. (As filled in by a husband who wanted to make his good wife happier.)

The problem .... *To make my wife happier* ....

Here are the three things that should do it—

1. Let her use the telephone as much as she wants

He always objected to the size of the telephone bill— and she heeded him—but he decided not to kick anymore. They lived off in the country. He was away in the city all day. The telephone was her way of keeping in touch with her friends and her family. She was no hour-long converser. When he told her to use it all she wanted, his bill ran about $20 more a month.

2. Let her travel

She loved to travel. He decided to spend his vacations going off on a trip with her—and he encouraged her to take a two week winter vacation with her buddy. This worked out beautifully. She was either happily planning some new trip—or talking happily about the last one.

3. Let her buy plants

She liked to buy azaleas, iris roots, holly bushes, dwarf fruit trees—etc. *ad infinitum.* He used to ask her why she was always buying more of that stuff. Now he encouraged her in this "green thumb" activity.

The varieties of factors that enter into making one's spouse happier vary endlessly from case to case. This man knew from experience that these things were the things that mattered in making his wife happy.

When he became sympathetic to these activities he had a more contented wife—who in turn made him happier and more contented. (Just incidentally, William James tells us not to be too critical of the little ways other people find their happiness.)

The next page shows how a man used
this technique to get feeling better.

Specimen form. (As used by a man who wanted to get himself feeling better physically.)

The problem .... *To get feeling better physically* ....

(*Background.* This man was not sick. The doctor found nothing wrong with him. But he felt below par and wanted to get feeling better.)

He tended to think too much about health and health rules and was always trying this new thing and that. He wondered if he should drink more water—or have more vitamins and minerals— or cut out desserts, etc., etc.

Then one day he impatiently asked himself, "What have I found from experience makes me feel better? Never mind the little things that might matter some. What are the few things that make a big difference?"

He decided that these three were the big things that matter:

1. Eat a light lunch

He always felt good when he stuck to a light lunch (some oatmeal cookies, an apple, black coffee).

2. Smoke only in the evening

Whenever he laid off cigarettes in the day he felt an immediate lift. He'd still smoke three or four cigarettes in the evening. Whenever he cut them out entirely he was always thinking of the fact that he wasn't smoking. He felt, everything considered, he was better off smoking a few.

3. Lay off the drinks

He liked to have two or three drinks every night before dinner—but when he cut them out he found (as Samuel Pepys found when he cut out wine) that he found himself much better. He would still drink on occasion and then limit himself to three drinks.

These were the things that this man knew from experience mattered to him. This is no blanket prescription. This was what worked for this man. It changed his life.

Form for your use.

For the "Few Things That Matter" Technique

The problem ....

Here are the few things that matter:

1. ....
....

2. ....
....

3. ....
....

4. ....
....

You can use this technique in any area, for any kind of problem, any kind of situation. Try it for a week. Try reducing things to their few essentials. See how it immediately increases your capacity. See how it launches you off to the kind of life that you want.

Want opportunities? They're all around you. Turn to the next action and see a technique that will give you more than you can handle.

To give you
a continuous supply
of rich opportunities

The purpose of this action is to uncover a tremendous new source of rich opportunities.

Here's the technique:

Whenever you hear anyone complain about anything, ask yourself this question: "What opportunity is hidden within this complaint?"

Opportunities by the score

Almost every complaint anyone makes (including yourself) carries an exciting opportunity right along with it. The complaint is only one side of the coin. Turn the coin over—and there, more often than not—is a juicy opportunity of one kind or another for the person imaginative enough to perceive it.

We must keep cocked a shrewd calculating ear to crabbing of any kind, be ready to pounce upon it as though it were loaded with opportunity. It probably is.

Three Kinds of Complaining

For the purposes of this discussion we are going to consider three kinds of complaining—three kinds we hear every day from others or from ourselves.

The first category of complaining

This category deals with our own crabbing and complaining—with little personal things that nettle us. These are loaded with potential opportunity—opportunity to get rid of nasty little situations that annoy us and at the same time to break through to a whole new approach for handling the more important problems that bother us.

For example: A man was always mislaying his keys—and he'd been doing it for years. He'd go muttering all through the house hunting for them, looking through his coats in the closet, going from mantlepiece to kitchen cabinet, looking in drawers. One day he decided he had had enough of this nonsense. He screwed a hook on the wall alongside the kitchen door and as soon as he came into the house he'd hang his keys there. This simple move saved him so much trouble that it pointed up the value of using this "something can be done about it" approach for *anything* that bothered him.

I know how utterly trivial this sounds, but many people continually face such annoying situations and do nothing about them but complain.

Are you your own friend or your enemy?

Montaigne says that a man has so many enemies that he can't afford to be his own. When a man is given an opportunity to make things easier for himself and he refuses to take advantage of it, he is certainly his own worst enemy. Virtually every time we kick about some little thing that annoys us there is inherent in the situation the chance to make something easier for ourselves.

One young man I know had a typewriter that used to jam up on him every few minutes. His train of thought would be broken; his anger made things worse. He'd grumble to himself—but would do nothing to correct the trouble. One day he stopped and tried to solve the problem. He fixed it in two seconds with a drop of oil.

Have you noticed how much more prone we are to complain than to take action to correct the thing we complain about? But here's a tremendous opportunity—if we will only use this dynamic technique—if we will ask ourselves this question every time we crab about anything: "What opportunity is hidden within this complaint?"

Remember, these opportunities are double-barrelled

Remember that a right about face in the way we react to these pesky little annoyances not only gives us the immediate benefit of removing the thing that annoys us, but it can be the opening wedge that leads to a change in our whole attitude in handling the bigger things that are bothering us. It can change our lives.

The second category of complaints— gripes about our jobs

Most everyone gripes about his job once in a while. Some gripe all the time. But here, above all, we must turn the coin over. There's rich opportunity spelled out on the other side—not only the opportunity to get rid of the condition we kick about, but an opportunity to distinguish ourselves in doing it.

This technique was all the old guy needed

A few years ago some 20 bright young men worked for an older man in his sixties, a department head named Smith. He wasn't too bright and he was as corny as they come. He used a favorite cliché so often the young fellows smilingly referred to him among themselves as Cliché Smith.

Whenever any of the young men would complain to him about some unpleasant aspect of the job he would tell them with unself-conscious earnestness, "Look upon it as an opportunity. Look upon it as a challenge!" The young fellows, who looked upon themselves as sophisticated and mildly cynical, would smile patronizingly whenever they heard this cliché.

But the old fellow meant it with all his heart. His greatest strength lay in this belief. It enabled him—despite his limitations—to run a difficult department successfully, and it enabled him when he retired to start a business of his own and win immediate success in a very tough game.

He believed, yes, really believed, that every complaint contains a challenge and an exciting opportunity. The young sophisticates who worked for him would have been infinitely better off if their mental image of themselves had permitted them to adopt so "naive" a cliché for their own. It's loaded with practical power.

Why your gripes about your own job are "loaded"

When you complain about your job, about some aspect of it that goes against the grain, listen, and listen carefully to your own complaint. It's your chance to go to town. Remember that a complaint about your own job is right in your own back yard. It's in the area that you control, the little segment of the world where you can make your influence felt right off the bat.

Be thankful that you have something to complain about—a chance to show your stuff. The right attitude in such cases is pure magic. If you use the technique we recommend here—if every time you complain you ask yourself, "What opportunity is hidden within this complaint?"—if your attitude is one of "let's go to town on this situation," then you won't have to climb in the world— *you'll rise.*

A young man stops crabbing—starts rising

This young man held a medium-sized job with a big successful investment banking firm, and part of the job entailed a couple of hours of monotonous clerical work each day. He was so busy with his regular work that he resented this chore. He griped about it, kept up a running conversation with himself on how impossible it was.

Each day he had the monotonous task of copying off about a hundred items from slips and posting them on "credit sheets." Then these credit sheets were sent to another department where what he had written down was copied off in turn by someone else. All he did for a while was to resent this drudgery.

One day an old friend called him up for lunch. He and this friend had worked together for "Cliché Smith" a couple of years before. They discussed Cliché Smith and were amazed at his success in going into business for himself. They tried to joke about how corny the old duck was. But their humor had a hollow ring. Neither of them was doing too well.

When the young fellow got back to his office he couldn't get Cliché Smith out of his mind. Maybe the old guy was right. Maybe he had the right idea. Maybe he should look upon his complaint as a challenge. Maybe there was an exciting opportunity wrapped up inside it.

For the first time he did some hard thinking about the problem. He couldn't figure out why he had to copy off from slips a lot of stuff that the next department copied all over again from his work. The whole operation looked like waste motion. He told his boss about the waste motion. The boss explained, "You have to copy off all those items to balance the dollar figures in our department."

The young man had thought of that, too. "But isn't it true that if I posted just the *total* of all the items it would balance our department's figures?"

They worked out a simple change that got rid of the

waste motion. Under the new set-up he handled *one* entry a day instead of about a hundred. He wondered why someone had not questioned all this waste motion before. He discovered that the system had gotten started years before when there were just one or two items a day. Then it hadn't made any difference how so small an operation was handled. *The items had steadily increased in numbers over the years and no one had thought to question a custom that had been sanctified by time.*

He was given credit for the whole thing. He began to go places, salary-wise and job-wise—but the most significant change in him was his new stance toward anything he complained about. He asked himself, "What opportunity is hidden in this complaint?" He had quit being his own worst enemy. He had at last joined sides with himself. His life opened up with a roar.

My job has no opportunity

This is one of the most common of all complaints, that the job you're in has no opportunity, that it has a salary ceiling, that you can't make any money at it or get anywhere in it. Years ago I complained to the brilliant Bill O'Hare that the advertising job I had was too limited, that I was tied up in job classification, salary ceiling and all that stuff.

He told me I was talking nonsense, that job classifications and salary ceilings are designed for average performance, that if a man does his job well enough he'll break through such artificial limitations one way or the other, that he'll even force a separate classification for himself if necessary, will create a special job for himself within the company.

When I turned the complaint coin over I saw the challenge spelled out on the other side. It said, "Go break the limitations on your job." And that's just what I did. I went at it hammer and tongs, made so much money for the company they worked out a separate classification for me. I broke the salary ceiling and went way on through it. I created a special spot for myself within the company.

When you chafe under your job's limitations, turn the coin over. Read the challenge and the opportunity written on the other side—"Break through those limitations! Create a unique spot for yourself!" Most companies are just as anxious to reward you for achievement as you are to gain it. And if they can't or won't, remember that a person of capacity and dedication never stays long in any job too small for him. There is no power on earth like the force of a dedicated individual. Something is bound to give somewhere.

And now the third category of complaints

This third group of complaints contains perhaps the hottest opportunities of all: the complaints *other people* make—things that people in general crab about. These complaints, if you'll only turn the coin over, can make you rich.

It's not the same place anymore

Have you heard all the kicking in recent years about how places everywhere are being spoiled by the crowds—things like "Long Island isn't Long Island anymore."

A few years ago many of us who lived in New York

City used to ride out on Long Island for our week-ends. My wife and I have known the Island all our lives, used to vacation there, and we love the place. But each time we'd go down the Island in recent years we were disappointed in seeing how crowded it had become. (I guess we wanted it to keep forever its earlier pastoral charm, to stay always the way it was when we were young.) Almost every one of us old-timers had the same gripe: "The place is overrun with people."

One of our friends used the technique I recommend here. He listened to all the complaining. He smiled and said nothing. He quietly turned the coin over. On the other side he saw his opportunity. He saw what was happening— that Long Island was in for terrific development and would be the site of scores of charming communities. He quietly bought himself a large tract of land for a couple of hundred dollars an acre and sold it a few short years later for ten times what he paid for it. This story, in one form or another, was endlessly repeated by people who did something more than crab about how crowded this place, or that place, was becoming.

And our colleges are so crowded

How are we going to use our technique here? Should we all go out and start colleges? For some very few people this of course will be the answer—but when we turn this coin over we see not just one opportunity but many.

For example: In this morning's mail I received a survey from one of the leading investment advisory houses in which they tell of the excellent opportunities offered by the stocks of certain publishing companies, companies that should profit from the boom in education, companies that publish textbooks. This looks like a very inviting picture. People who listened five years ago to all the complaining about crowded schools and colleges and invested at that time in these publishing companies have already seen their investment multiplied as much as ten times over.

And all the crabbing about crowded colleges suggests the enormous opportunities there are in "study by mail." That field is expected to increase in dollar volume from $50,000,000 a year to over a billion in the next few years—to multiply 20 times over.

Make this technique standard procedure

We must make this technique standard procedure. When people crab and complain—when they grouse and carp—whether it's about cars being too big, or eating places being unsatisfactory, or places getting too crowded—no matter what the complaint—let's turn the coin over and see what opportunity is spelled out on the other side. Here is a way to keep yourself supplied with a continuous stream of fresh opportunities.

But most important of all is the change that this technique can foster in us—the changed attitude that comes to us when we apply this technique to all our own complaining—and the complaining we hear from others. It leads us to take a dynamic new approach to *all kinds* of situations—a positive approach bristling with vital constructive energy. When we make this technique of turning the complaint coin over part and parcel of our method of operation, we start to move immediately toward achievement and happiness—no longer clawing and climbing our way up—but rising, rising by the natural power of this buoyant technique.

On the next page is a list of hints for using this terrific technique.

Then there are specific examples of the complaints a man heard from himself and from others—and what he did about them.

Then there are three simple forms for you to use in capitalizing on the three different categories of complaints that you hear (as outlined in the foregoing chapter).

Hints for Using This Technique That Turns Complaints Into Opportunities

1. More often than not when anyone complains about anything there's an opportunity wrapped up in the complaint.

2. Listen when you yourself kick about little "personal" things that get your goat. When you act to correct these annoyances you not only get rid of the bother, but it can touch off a whole new attitude for the constructive handling of all sorts of things that bother you.

3. Listen when other people complain about situations. Make it standard procedure to turn the coin over—see what opportunity is spelled out on the other side.

4. Remember that when we refuse to do anything but complain about things that bother us we perpetuate an endless cycle of frustration.

5. Get things out of your system by crabbing about things first if you must—but then ask yourself, "How can I capitalize on this?"

6. When something about your job doesn't suit you, be sure to turn the coin over. Here's your chance to go to town in an area that you yourself control.

7. Remember, there is not just one opportunity on the other side of the coin—there are often several.

Three exciting illustrations follow, showing this technique in action—how a man made tremendous capital out of the little things in his personal life that got his goat, out of the things he complained about in his job —out of the complaints he heard from other people.

Three Lists of Complaints as Made Out
by a 35-Year-Old $9,000 Minor Executive

Form 1—For the first category of complaints. He wrote down annoyances in his personal life—things about which he had only complained.

Annoyance 1   The window in the bedroom stuck every night when he tried to open it. He muttered to himself about it—said it would give him a hernia.

Action   He loosened up the frame of the tracks on the window with a screwdriver—and then he smeared soap on them. This took ten minutes and it worked easily from then on.

Annoyance 2   A couple of mornings each week a neighbor's dog would come around at daybreak and bark for an hour—driving them crazy—costing them a couple of hours of much needed sleep. They groused about it for months—did nothing.

Action   He hesitated to take action—but knew that he must. He called on the neighbors, found them decent people. They said they were sorry and would keep the dog at home. They heard him only twice in the year that followed.

Annoyance 3   The windshield wiper blades on his car were so worn that every time it rained he would have to slump way down in the seat to find a clear spot to look through. This had annoyed him a dozen times—and he had grumbled about it, but had failed to get new ones.

Action   One day—shortly after he had been sold on this "don't complain, do something" technique—it began to rain as he was driving along. He pulled into the next gas station he came to and had the blades replaced.

As soon as he stopped complaining and started to take action on the things that bothered him he gained an immediate benefit. The things themselves were cleared up—but he had released an infinitely bigger thing within him. These little actions had thrown things wide open—fostered the taking of dynamic constructive action on his "main-arena" problems.

Form 2—For the second category of complaints. He wrote down his complaints about his job—things about which he had done nothing.

Here were his complaints—and the action that turned these complaints into triumphs:

Complaint 1 He was interrupted all day long by people who worked for him coming in to see him.

Action He set aside a five-minute period each day for each of the seven people in his department—told them to come in with questions written down. This not only saved him time—but immediately firmed up everybody's performance.

Complaint 2 The company was filled with bad feeling. Most everyone was sore at everyone else—unpleasant, unco-operative.

Action He'd capitalize on it—try to make his desk an oasis of civility. This worked magic for him. His pleasant courtesy immediately got him better service in everything he needed—and it ended his own resentments which had been eating him up.

Complaint 3 Whenever he turned down a piece of work from one of the writers in the department, they were angry and hurt—like children.

Action He'd use an entirely different approach—enlist their vanity, get them excitedly cooperating to turn out electric, dynamic copy. He'd tell them that this thing they have written up suggests such a great potential, let's go all out on it and make it a sockeroo. Then he would talk with them about making it a GREAT piece of copy—and how they could do it. It set them on fire.

Remember that in your gripes about your job there's no end of rich opportunity. Turn the coin over. What looks like a negative discouraging situation is just the tail of the coin. Here is potential triumph—the chance to go gloriously to town.

This is, of course, an illustration taken from business—but the things that work in business have been tried in the crucible. Business uses a technique because it works. This technique works anywhere and everywhere.

Form 3—For the third category of complaints. He wrote down some of the complaints he heard from other people.

The list below contains just three of the complaints others made—and how he took action to make capital out of them:

Complaint 1 Vitamins cost too much.

Action He, too, had quite a vitamin bill for his children. He had heard so many gripes about this that he kept turning the coin over. And there it was. He remembered that the family doctor had told them about a place in the city where you could buy good vitamins at a fraction of their cost. On his next trip in he'd save himself a $10 bill.

Complaint 2 I get too much junk mail—too much advertising. He was in the advertising business and people liked to complain to him about all the cheap-looking stuff he—and other people sent them.

Action If they were getting so much stuff that looked like junk —he'd send them something that wouldn't look like junk. He thought up the idea of sending out mail in a "securities envelope" —something called a "red wallet." It looked as though it contained the most important stuff ever trusted to the mails. This made hundreds of thousands of dollars for him. He had turned the complaint coin over and cleaned up.

Complaint 3 Can't find an apartment at a decent price.

Action This was a very important complaint for him. Listening to it and turning the coin over solved a sticky problem for him.

A few years before, his wife had inherited from her grandfather a run-down three-family house. It needed complete renovation—was boarded up and unoccupied. They gave the place an inexpensive facelifting—sold it to a man who wanted to live in one apartment and rent the other two. Every complaint is an opportunity for someone. Turn the coin over.

Listen to every complaint you hear. When you hear a complaint all the time it points to an opportunity. Use your imagination and resourcefulness to make capital of them.

Most people are content to complain just to get things out of their systems—but you can use them to go to town.

Form 1 (for your use).

List here the pesky little things that annoy you—and the action you're going to take to get rid of them.

Annoyance 1 ....

    Action to take ....

....

Annoyance 2 ....

    Action to take ....

....

Annoyance 3 ....

    Action to take ....

....

Annoyance 4 ....

    Action to take ....

....

Annoyance 5 ....

    Action to take ....

....

Little pesky annoyances are loaded with opportunity—to get rid of the annoying condition itself—and as a door-opener to a dynamic constructive approach for handling all kinds of problems.

Form 2 (for your use).

List below your gripes about your job and figure out the action you can take to turn them into triumph.

Complaint 1 ....

    Action to take ....

....

Complaint 2 ....

    Action to take ....

....

Complaint 3 ....

    Action to take ....

....

Complaint 4 ....

    Action to take ....

....

Complaint 5 ....

    Action to take ....

....

Remember that your complaints about your job are regular bomb-shells of opportunity. Here's a close-at-hand opportunity to distinguish yourself. Turn the coin over. Go to town.

Form 3 (for your use).

List below the complaints you hear from others—analyze them—
see the hidden opportunities within them. Here's where this technique can literally pour benefits into your life. List below the action
you'll take to capitalize on these complaints.

Complaint 1 ....

    Action to take ....
....

Complaint 2 ....

    Action to take ....
....

Complaint 3 ....

    Action to take ....
....

Complaint 4 ....

    Action to take ....
....

Complaint 5 ....

    Action to take ....
....

These complaints you hear from others are an inexhaustible source
of opportunity—opportunity for financial gain, ideas for your job
—situations that point to endless benefits for the person who
knows how to use them.

*Now let's turn to the richest chapter in the whole
book—the action for launching out from right where
you are today—and into a glorious life.*

To improve
your circumstances rapidly
no matter what they are

This dynamic technique enables you to move fast out of your present circumstances and into better things.

Here's the technique:

Map out a one-day program that calls for going all-out on your current set-up *whether you like the set-up or not.*

Here's the background explanation:

Many people are bogged down in a life they don't like. They don't like their jobs—they don't like their associates—they're unhappy about their financial condition, the place they have to live, their social life, their home life. The sad thing is *not* that these people dislike their circumstances—but their stance toward their set-ups is all wrong—that their wrong attitude keeps them hopelessly locked up in conditions that are so distasteful to them.

We have no quarrel with anyone who's dissatisfied—but it's one thing to be dissatisfied with your environment and another thing to refuse to use it. The thing that causes our unhappiness is this: we will not use today because it doesn't suit us. This resistance to reality utterly paralyzes our powers. It ties us hand and foot. Every life process within us is geared to present circumstances no matter what those circumstances are. If you refuse to act within your "here and now" you cut your contact with your only source of power.

But here's the haymaker:

> You gain immediate power to change your circumstances when *for just one day* you act with force on the situation in which you find yourself whether you like the facts of it or not.

Bill—a common example of resisting reality

Bill has a measly little job and he's perfectly justified in being dissatisfied with it. He's bright (IQ 142)—he's educated (top college)—he has a good imagination—and he makes a crisp appearance. But Bill's attitude toward his job is poison. He's not only dissatisfied with it (which is O.K.), but he refuses to use it (which is disastrous). Instead of using his "lousy little job" as a starting point to get the life force flowing through him, he turns his back on it, spurns it. Because he doesn't like it, he won't use it—and he must use it if he's going to change it, or even move out of it.

Bill is correspondent for the company at $4,500 a year. His job is answering letters of complaint. The job consists of choosing the right letter from among 12 form letters, making the appropriate changes in the form letter chosen, and then dictating the finished product into a Dictaphone. Bill told me that he had had this little job for two years. The night he talked with me about it he had just put in an impossibly boring day. I asked him if he had resigned at the end of such a miserable day. He looked at me wide-eyed and said, "One doesn't simply give up a job."

If you didn't resign you decided to stay

I told Bill, "Of course one doesn't simply give up a job, but when you didn't resign the job, it meant, whether you realize it or not, that your decision was to stay on it. As long as you're on this job and refuse to use it there can be no life force in you."

The number one problem for most people is to find some way to get themselves to make use of things as they are today whether they like them or not. This can make you or break you. Without this realism you're "oomphless." Without this realism the mechanisms that supply you with energy, that fill you with hope, that give meaning to life, simply aren't running. I gave Bill the following simple example:

Think of yourself in your present set-up as a person standing on a step in a flight of stairs. You don't like the step you're standing on—and it's O.K. not to like the step that you're on—but if you're going to get off that step you have to use that step *for the purpose of moving off it*. It must support your weight as you push yourself off it.

What you're doing is refusing to acknowledge the fact that you're standing on that step and as long as you resist that fact you're going to be stuck on it.

Tough realists always make use of their environments whether they like them or not. They don't let themselves get bogged down in something *just because they don't like it*.

Relief in a matter of hours

As soon as a person says to himself, "This is where I am today; my only salvation lies in acting where I am," things change fast. (Where else, in heaven's name, can a person act if not within things as they are?) As soon as he starts working for one day with his "here and now," a seeming miracle takes place. Life starts coursing through him, hope comes rushing in, exciting goals for the future replace one's grim forebodings. The whole picture is changed.

So what do I have to lose?

Bill was so miserable he said he'd take a crack at anything that might help him. He shrugged, smiled wanly and said, "So what do I have to lose?" But as soon as he made this decision he began to feel better—half-hearted as his decision seemed to be. It began to pump strength into him. His grip, his hold, firmed up by the minute as he sat there. He said, "All right, I'll start right where I am, do what I can with things as they are."

He made up a one-day program that called for going all-out on his job—for handling it with intelligence and vigor.

Bill wakes up

For the first time in two years Bill asked himself what the company was trying to achieve through his job. For the first time in two years he carefully read the 12 letters he'd been using every day. He wanted to see how well they suited their purpose. He found one of the letters so shockingly bad he took it to his department head and told him how bad it was. The department head, a mouth-breathing lightweight, told him in bad English and with worse grace: "If it don't suit you, write a better one."

And Bill wrote a better one. He worked on it for hours one evening, writing it and rewriting it till he had a letter that sounded completely reasonable, was a masterpiece of tact, a letter that was smooth as butter, a letter that left the complainer better pleased with himself and well disposed toward the company.

Bill's whole inner machinery sprang electrically to life as soon as for one day he became fully engaged with his "here and now." He soon got caught up on his work which had always been a week or more behind. Complaints were being answered the day they came in and they were being answered well. He was doing his job, using his energy and brains in it.

Bill solves his problem

This changed attitude turned Bill overnight from a weak malcontent into a strong man. It made him a realist, a dynamic realist. But here's the payoff. For the first time in the two years he had held his job *he felt free to take steps to get out of it.* His new attitude had cleared the decks for action. He was ready to solve his problem, to get out of his department.

He knew just what he was going to do—and a couple of days later he did it. He called up the advertising manager of the company, asked if he could see him. He showed him the letter he had written, told him he'd like to work for him. The advertising manager read the letter and talked with him for 15 minutes (sizing him up) and then told Bill he'd think about it. A week later Bill was transferred to the advertising department. His job classification changed; his salary was immediately increased. He and the ad manager hit it off right from the start. (The ad manager was a brilliant man and a treat to work with after his old boss.) He loved the new job, felt this was where he belonged—but here's the whole point: His all-out acceptance of the old job was the key that opened the new one. He *used* the old job to get out of it and into something he liked.

Maybe you don't need to change jobs

Maybe you don't need a new job. Maybe all you need to find yourself a terrific success is to give your current set-up the full treatment. That's what Mildred did, and her life burst forth into happiness and success. But she got nowhere till she stopped fighting her "here and now."

Mildred is a librarian. She has the talents to make a top librarian, but she wouldn't bring them into play. She's vain (which means she's concerned with the figure she cuts in other people's minds)—but it wasn't vanity as such that hurt her. Vanity can serve as a sharp spur to bring one's powers into play, but Mildred was so uppity and so vain about her talents that she refused to use them in her little library job.

Mildred thinks of herself as a highly creative person (and it's true she has talent and imagination—not quite as much as she feels the need to think she has—yet she is way above average). Mildred wanted to do something more dramatic, more striking than library work. She turned her back on her library set-up, would have nothing to do with her "today"—or no more than she had to in order to get by. She told herself that she'd begin to live when things were different for her. She wouldn't even use the step she was standing on in order to get off it. This attitude cut off her contact with her own life force. She refused to have any truck with the only reality anyone can know, which is the set-up in which one finds one's self today.

Mildred was unhappy as only a person can be who is practicing the grandest of all deceptions, the grand deception of believing she was an exception to the rule that everyone must live in the present—if he's going to live at all.

This grand deception which Mildred practiced because she thought she was too wonderful for her library job made her miserable, as only a king-sized deception can. Her extreme unhappiness was shouting to her to tell her she had the wrong slant on things. It was meant to serve as a corrective, to force her to change, to get her to start functioning within her "here and now."

In the Bible (*Ecclesiastes IX, 10*) there is this verse:

> Whatsoever thy hand findeth to do, do it
> with thy might.

There never was a sounder admonition for Mildred—and for you and me. The path to fulfillment of your powers *leads off* from things at hand.

Mildred likes Emerson

One evening when I stopped at the library desk to check out some books I got to talking with Mildred. She told me again, as she had so often in the past, that she was fed up with library work, didn't know what she ought to do. She noticed that one of the books I was taking out was about Emerson. She mentioned in passing how much she liked his writings. She said he talked sense.

"If you go along with Emerson," I said, "you shouldn't have too much trouble deciding what to do."

"What do you mean?"

"Doesn't he say somewhere to 'spend yourself on the work before you'?"

"Yes, he does." She smiled. "Maybe someday I'll try it."

"Why not try it tomorrow? Just for one day. Give this library job everything you've got. See what happens. My guess is that things will open for you pretty quick."

Mildred maps out a plan

Mildred mapped out a plan that called for one day's total engagement with her job. It threw open the floodgates of life. Her one day of realistic action not only changed her attitude, it dramatically changed her life. Before the first day was over she decided no longer to save her creative powers till she got into something that offered them greater opportunity for expression. She'd use them right where she was. Her biggest surprise came in finding scores of opportunities for her precious creativity right in the library that she had always thought of as just "a drab little dump."

And she got some hot new ideas

As soon as her attitude changed she got some hot new ideas for her job. She dreamed up a series of book displays for the library—displays on subjects currently in the news. She painted the posters for these displays (and they were uncommonly good posters). She used excellent judgment in choosing a dozen books on each subject and featured them ingeniously in table displays. These projects were done so well they were the talk of the town.

Maybe it won't work the same way for you— but it will work

Mildred found she liked her library job, that she didn't need to get into something different in order to find satisfaction. She found that things improve fast when one tries to bring one's capacities into play, when one does the best one can right where one is.

All Mildred needed was a change in attitude in order to be happy—but it may not work out in just the same way for you. Maybe you'll need to change your environment, too, but you can't even begin to change it unless you stop resisting it and start using it—just as it is.

Fred does an about face—
skyrockets from failure to success

Fred suffered from the most common disease of our day—hurt feelings. He was always in a stew, fretting over how someone had hurt him. If there was nothing fresh to fret about he would dredge things up out of the distant past and relive them, dwell on how someone had hurt him ten years ago, remember how he had spoken to someone and the person had not even answered him.

Fred was trying to duck reality

Fred's big trouble was that he was in total resistance to his environment on all fronts. He would not accept and go to work on any aspect of his life the way it was. He wanted nothing to do with the "piddling limitations of his set-up"—with the small-time job in the purchasing department of his company—with the "sub-mediocre" people he worked with—with the "dynamic morons" who were his neighbors. The thing that undid him was this:

> He could not face the thought of buckling down and accepting his circumstances, even for the purpose of using them in order to change them, or even for using them in order to get completely out of them.

He insisted that he was fit for a much better job, which he was, or would have been if he would only have become engaged with the stuff of his "here and now"—the stuff all life is made of. It's the engagement of ourselves with that stuff, no matter what it is, that starts the life force flowing again, and it's the only action that can start it.

Like everyone else who tries to duck reality, who resists the facts of his situation and refuses to become engaged with them, Fred paid for it and Fred paid for it by a painful sensitiveness to the way others treated him. Nature is very quick to show us that we're wrong when we turn our backs on our "here and now." She jabs a pin into us and with a wonderful economy she jabs it into our most sensitive spot. Fred had the tendency to be touchy and easily hurt and that's where Nature let him have it.

Another person, who, let's say, was prone to worry about money matters, would have gotten the pin there and been worried about losing his job. But you're going to get it somewhere if you try to resist your circumstances. You either live today—or you're unhappy about something.

But my set-up is terrible

Fred spilled out his whole story one evening when he called at my place. (He was a pretty good friend of mine, a young fellow with whom I struck up an acquaintance a few years back when we worked in the same outfit.) I told him he should stop fighting his environment and start using it—whether he liked it or not. He looked very unhappy and said that his set-up was terrible.

"Nobody's arguing that it's not terrible. You don't have to accept it with open arms. You're not going to live with it the rest of your life—but you must stop fighting it, be realistic enough to use it, be willing for just one day to try all-out engagement with it."

Fred is reluctant—but he tries

Fred said, all right, he'd try it. He'd do the best he could with it for just one day. He made up a one-day program that called for going all-out on his "here and now," and he carried it out. (Fred's one-day program is given on page 243.) He took care of everything that came along—used his head on things—was a little grim and angry about everything at first—but was working within the framework of his circumstances. He had come into contact with the only life anyone can know—the life of one's "here and now."

Fred gets three tremendous benefits right off the bat

This one-day program broke Fred's life wide open—changed everything for him in a matter of hours. The self-righting automatic mechanisms began functioning again within him—the mechanisms that guide us, that turn on the energy, that integrate us, that liberate us and fill us with hope as soon as we stop fighting our today and start to use it.

These three things happened to him:

1. Before the first day was over he began to feel hopeful about the future. An exciting goal began to take shape in his mind. (He had always wanted to do something with salesmen—to teach them and inspire them—and he saw a way to get this going *today*.) Fred found what everyone else finds—that hopeful goals for the future rise rapidly out of full engagement with the present.

2. He became more independent—stopped trying to conciliate everyone. He was working with reality, and realists don't worry too much what others think about them—nor nervously try to appease them.

3. He stopped reliving his unhappy experiences from the past—he stopped worrying about the future. He found that the way to break with the past—and with the future—is to start acting in your present—no matter what it is.

We're not talking about "adjustment"

Some of us value our uniqueness so highly that we're afraid we'll lose that uniqueness if we start applying ourselves to our environment—no matter what it is—and without regard to how well it suits our talents. We feel that if we *adjust* we will lose our precious individuality.

People who follow this disastrous line will quote the great Emerson to you as their justification. Didn't he say to us, "Insist on yourself"?

Emerson is in a sense the father of us all. Our debt to him is enormous. He shows us that the way to live is to be yourself and at all costs to realize the individuality within you. But many unhappy people misunderstand him and think that his philosophy justifies their not taking action when conditions are not right for giving expression to their unique talents. They forget, or perhaps they mean to forget, that Emerson also said:

> Sufficient to today are the duties of today. Don't waste life in doubts and fears; spend yourself on the work before you, well assured that the right performance of this hour's duties will be the best preparation for the hours or ages that follow it.

We are all seeking an ever increasing personal fulfillment. We wish to pursue ever more meaningful goals with our own special talents enjoying full play. But the road to such a life *starts off* from the conditions in which we find ourselves today. Stop fighting your "here and now." Start using it just as it is today—no matter what it is. It's the way to liberate the true self. It's constructive realism.

On the next few pages are the material and forms you need to bring the "miracle" of "here and now" dramatically into play.

Ten Hints for Using the Dynamite of Here and Now

1. Stop fighting your current set-up. It's the only reality there is.

2. Just for one day do what you can with your life as it is —with your job, your home life, with everything in your environment.

3. You don't have to find a formula that will solve all your problems for the rest of your life—all you have to do is to do what you can to make today good.

4. For example: Just for today, follow the health rules that you know make you feel better. Don't try to find a formula for lifelong health.

5. If you must be vain (and most people must), be vain about how realistic you are. The test of realism is in not resisting your here and now.

6. Remember that the life forces can work within you only as you live within today's conditions. Start the juice of life flowing through you by acting vigorously on things that are "at hand."

7. Nobody says you've got to like your current conditions —but you've got to use them—even to get out of them.

8. Hope rushes in when you stop fighting with reality. Positive thinking is the result of this realism.

9. So you want to find fulfillment. But remember that the road to fulfillment *leads off* from action on things as they are today.

10. *Important:* Write down a one-day program that calls for action on things as they are in your set-up "here and now." (Sample filled-in program follows and then a form for you to use in making out your own one-day program.)

Sample One-Day Program
of
Fred M. . . . .

(The young man who fretted
over hurt feelings.)

Quick picture of Fred

Fred is 28 years old. He's a very minor boss in his company's purchasing department. He's resisting his job—wants to be free from it—would like to do something like train and inspire salesmen—but his attitude toward his present job has paralyzed in him the power to take action on getting the kind of job he wants.

His personal relationship with the people around him makes him continuously unhappy. He alternates in his treatment of them between a weak ingratiation and a testy arrogance.

Here is Fred's one-day program (made up the evening before):

1. Tell myself when I get out of bed in the morning I don't have to make my whole life good—just today.

2. Instead of getting to work 15 minutes late—I'm going to get in a half-hour earlier.

3. Tomorrow I'm going to see our own company salesmanager and show him those sample brief cases he wants for our own salesmen. (He asked for them six weeks ago and I've been putting it off.)

4. If at any time during the day I feel resentment toward my boss (and I'm pretty sure I will), I'll tell myself that this won't bother me if I attack my "here and now."

5. I'll try not to be annoyed when two dozen people within the company call me up—all wanting something in a hurry. I'll give them all the help I can.

6. No more two-hour lunches with salesmen who are trying to sell me something. This is a waste of time, and after two martinis and a heavy lunch I feel sunk.

7. From now on I'll see salesmen only by appointment—but I'll see anyone who wants to see me. When a salesman phones for an appointment, I'll ask him to be ready to make his point in five minutes—and when he comes I'll jot down the point. (I've been missing some good bets in trying to brush them off.)

8. I'll read that magazine article that shows seven ways a purchasing agent can save money for his company.

Fred comes through

Before the first day was over this simple one-day program had launched Fred off on an exciting new life. When he went to see the company salesmanager about those brief cases late that afternoon, his new attitude gave him the courage to tell the salesmanager something he had been thinking about for months. Fred suggested to him that he be permitted to give a talk to the company salesmen on how to sell to purchasing agents—based on his own experience as a purchasing agent.

Fred's talk was a bombshell. In three months he was instructing salesmen for the company. In two years he had his own sales consulting business—was going around giving talks to sales groups. He was tops in this business, in demand everywhere. He had become successful and happy—and the whole change in Fred's life started with the above one-day program.

Now turn to the next page and fill in your own one-day program.

Form for your use.

Use this form for filling in your own one-day program for going all out on your "here and now."

(This can cover action on your job—your home life—social life—or any aspect of your current situation.)

Date . . . .

I'm going to do the following tomorrow:

1. . . . .
. . . .

2. . . . .
. . . .

3. . . . .
. . . .

4. . . . .
. . . .

5. . . . .
. . . .

6. . . . .
. . . .

7. . . . .
. . . .

8. . . . .
. . . .

245

You'll do better with this program if you fill it in at home the night before. Your program should call for action—total engagement with the stuff of your "here and now."

Don't go off the deep end—don't upset the apple cart. Just stop resisting the realities of your set-up and do the best you can with it.

This poem below is one of the finest I have ever read and it backs up so beautifully the point I'm trying to make in this chapter that I want you to be sure to read it.

It's as old as the hills—originally written in Sanskrit. It supports this chapter with the "sifted wisdom of the ages."

The Challenge

Listen to the exhortation of the dawn!
    Look to this day!
For it is life, the very life of life.
In its brief course lie all the verities
And realities of your existence:
The glory of action, the bliss of growth,
The splendor of beauty:
For yesterday is but a dream.
And tomorrow is only a vision;
But today, well lived, makes
Every yesterday a dream of happiness
And every tomorrow a vision of hope.
Look well, therefore, to this Day!
Such is the salutation of the Dawn.

Now turn to the next few pages for the closing bombshell—the most powerful message in this powerful book.

You can change things — FAST!

This book can change your life—and change it with incredible speed. Its extraordinary power lies in its Program for Action—a program of specific actions to open your life with a bang.

These specific actions are the heart of the whole book—the reasons for its enormous success. They are not like other actions. They're triggers, triggers that set off terrific powers within you—the very powers you need for vital, victorious living. The book is *not* a philosophical discussion. It's built entirely around these "key actions," actions that have the power to change things for you virtually overnight.

Dramatically effective as these actions are, they are utterly realistic. They don't promise something for nothing. But they do release the energy, the confidence, the capacity you need to get the things you want—and to get them faster than you've ever dreamed possible.

How fast does this program really work?

The title promises a new life in ten days. Does it really work that fast? Actually it works much faster. Any one of these actions can change things at once. Power is released as soon as you touch it.

For example: Suppose, like many people, you need more confidence. You take the action given. (Make a specific promise to yourself—see Part II, Action 1.) The minute you take this action (as directed) it begins to release power. These actions work so fast that I at one time considered naming the book "Actions for Instant Living"—but the "Instant Living" had a frivolous ring and to someone unfamiliar with the exciting program the book contains it would sound like a silly exaggeration. But any one of these actions does have an instantaneous effect and the whole program can be brought into play within a week or ten days. Some of the actions take almost no time at all—some of them take a few minutes a day—a few of them take a bit longer. But as soon as you touch any part of this Program it starts releasing surging new power. You don't have to wait ten days to get this power. You get it at once.

These actions work for everybody

These actions are loaded with power for anyone and everyone. They work their "magic" for men, for women, for executives, for young men starting their careers, for professional people, for housewives, for women in business, for company presidents. They are built around basic principles—principles which are least common denominators in everyone's existence.

One company president—when he read this book—said what he liked about it was this: that many of the examples showing the power of these actions were taken from business life. He said that this proved their power to him—

that nothing is more realistic and practical than business. If they work in business they meet the acid test. They'll work anywhere. They're founded on principles that cut across the board into every life. They'll work for anyone.

This is a desk manual for living—not a book to be read once

Don't make the mistake of treating this like just an ordinary book—something to be read once and then forgotten. It's meant to be used as a guide—as a "desk manual" —something you keep alongside you for constant use. Remember that its enormous power lies in the specific actions it gives you to perform, and in the "blueprint-for-action" pages at the end of each chapter (where you carry out the action).

Read and reread the book. Take these releasing actions. Feel the new surge of power as you perform each one. The more you use this program, the more power it releases, the more you'll want to use it. Keep the book handy for coping with special problems as they arise. Suppose you're suddenly faced with making a tough decision. Turn to Part III, Action 3—and there is the specific action to multiply your power to form a wise decision. The book gives a specific action for releasing virtually any kind of power you may need. Keep it always on hand, always ready for such emergencies.

In what order shall I take on these actions?

You can take on the book as a "crash program" and get every one of these actions working for you in a week. This will take about an hour a night. But there may be one area in which you particularly want help. Maybe the thing you need most is to release your wealth-building capacity—and perhaps the thing you need most in this department is to build "financial drive" in yourself. Then you simply turn to Part IV, Action 1, entitled "To give you financial drive" and take the simple action that speedily builds up this drive within you.

A very busy man may get best results with the program by taking on one new action every three days and get the whole thing going in 30 days.

One advertising man found the method given for releasing the inner mind's capacity for coming up with ideas was the thing he needed most and he went straight to Part III, Action 1, and set himself on fire with a blaze of ideas ten times as great as he had been getting.

A young man who was in rebellion against his set-up, and trapped in that set-up by his own unrealistic attitude toward it, found the last action in the book the thing he needed most to turn on his power.

A person who tends to be an old fogey and over-fussy about details will find the action (Part V, Action 1) that will give him the big man's perspective.

But there is a definite reason for the order in which these actions appear in the book. They start logically with the action of "writing down your goals" in the Goal-A-Graph (at the close of the first action)—and then take you right through the actions that release the electric qualities you need to achieve those goals. Many people will find that following the order in which they are given in the book is the most effective method for taking on this Program for Action.

The utter realism of this book

Every person must be a realist first and last. You've got to work with things as they are. Here is the last word in realism, the realism of specific action NOW—of taking action on things *as they are*. The weakness of many well-educated people is this: They separate learning from life, carry around their learning in a separate compartment, isolated from today. You can know a score of subjects academically, be able to discuss a thousand books—and still be ineffective. The reason is simply this: Such people are locked within the "circle of knowing" and until they can move into the "circle of doing" they are without practical power. Here is where this book comes crashing through. It gives you *not just action*—it gives you not just *specific action*—it gives you *the specific actions* that release your powers. It enables you to launch out from right where you are, from things as they are today. It makes you a realist—and a realist filled with hope. This book is a powerhouse because it shows you how to achieve the two things necessary for triumphant living: (1) to bring your powers into play (2) within the framework of your current set-up. That's what gives this book such double-barrelled power. It enables you to release your talents starting with things as they are today. That realism is the heart of the actions in this book.

Life is meant to be an ecstasy

Emerson tells us that life should be an ecstasy—but how many of us find it so? Many of us find it anything but that. But we can change things. We can break through to rewarding, successful, happy living. For many of us this means an about-face—a whole new approach—new ways of looking at things—new thinking. But the actions given in this book bring about such changes. That's what makes this program great. The actions release the new powers we need to lead a new kind of life. Take the action and the rest tends automatically to follow.

You've got to get living

Remember that you've got to get living to be happy. As long as you're not giving expression to the kind of person you were meant to be you're going to spend your life justifying yourself to yourself and to others—or at least you'll spend your life *trying* to justify yourself. This is never any good. It means living your life as a kind of expiation for not being yourself—for not bringing that self into action. It means negative thinking of one kind or another. It means feeling resentment, being bitter, being anxious about the future—being bored, being discontented. And it's all so unnecessary. We can start living now—right off—within the framework of things as they are—if we will take these simple actions. Here is the path that will lead us into vital victorious days.

What do you want?

Do you want stimulating activity? Do you want money? Do you want success? A good job? Do you want to be free of too much concern with what others think of you? The path to these things starts off from the actions in this book. You can get just about anything you want if you will act—if you will seriously follow this exciting program.

I've seen these actions put people on the high road to life as soon as they touched them.

I've seen it make a woman a regular powerhouse for getting just the kind of home she always wanted.

I've seen one of these actions show a salesman his strong point and multiply his selling power by ten.

I've seen one of these actions give a man such self-belief, make him so rock-like in character that he easily dominated those around him.

I've seen one of these actions take a man who "never did any real thinking" and turn him into a person of towering good judgment.

I've seen one of these actions take a man who was running away from the kind of life he really wanted and turn him into one of the top men in his field.

I've seen how following one of these actions built one of the finest and most successful department stores in the country.

I've seen a man who was dead broke turn to one of these actions and send his income up to as high as $100,000 a year.

I've seen one of these actions enable a young man to make a few remarks at an executive meeting—so aptly, so forcefully—that he made himself known to the entire company.

I've seen one of these actions enable a person to come to a decision in three minutes on a situation he thought he never could cope with.

The line-up is endless—but the actions are quick and few. You perform them in minutes and the power they release goes rolling on and on. Remember that these actions bring material success—but that's not all they bring. They give you confidence. They make you feel adequate to your tasks (which is what happiness largely consists of). They make you self-determining so you can make plans and carry them out. They release your full mental powers. They give you the true basis of inner self-esteem. They enable you to find your hottest talents—let you feel the strength of these talents in action.

The program is complete—all worked out for you

Everything in this program has been worked out for you—reduced to the taking of a few specific actions. We have worked these actions into a complete formula for you, going so far as to supply ingenious forms at the end of each chapter for taking the specific action. You don't have to buy another thing to get started in any one of them. No stone has been left unturned to make the whole program simple for you to follow. We've done everything but take the actions for you. That is up to you.

Take these actions. They'll pay you back a thousand times for every bit of energy you expend in performing them. Invest a little time and a little energy in these actions and make the most fantastically exciting investment anyone can make. The rewards are incalculable. They pay off on a colossal scale. The whole thing is ready for you. The program for taking these actions is laid out like a blueprint —clear-cut, simple to follow.

What will it be for you?

Right now you have an enormous opportunity to open up your life, an opportunity to get over into the kind of life you want to lead. Give this book the full treatment. Live with it. Study it. Take its actions. Make the small effort required to put this electrifying program across in your life. Bring your greater capacities into action. You'll never find any joy till you live out your talents in action. You were meant to be a success—meant to be happy. You were meant to find your life a colorful, satisfying experience. You can go on living one tenth of the great life you were meant to live—or you can start living fully now—pursuing goals that set you on fire—filled with a confidence that sweeps everything before it—feeling the strength of your talents in action—with your mental powers in full swing—richly rewarded with material well-being—and working realistically with life as it is.

A large order?

Of course it's a large order—but it's an order you can fill if you will take the actions that open up your powers. You were meant to be successful, respected, at peace with yourself—to render the fine service to others that you are equipped by your nature to fulfill. You were meant for a glorious existence. And it all can be yours through the electric program of specific actions this book so excitingly presents.

On the next page are a few things to remember while using this book to get over into your great new life.

Begin Your New Life
NOW

Remember that all the great potential
power within you is useless unless you
can bring it to bear.

Remember that the special actions in
this book release your power—make it
available to you.

Remember there's a bigger, more successful, more satisfying life waiting right
here for you. Take these actions and make
it yours.

*The best of everything in the great
new life that lies before you.*

A PERSONAL WORD FROM MELVIN POWERS
PUBLISHER, WILSHIRE BOOK COMPANY

Dear Friend:

It is my sincere hope that you will find this catalog of more than passing interest because I am firmly convinced that one (or more) of the books herein contains exactly the information and inspiration you need to achieve goals you have previously thought were unattainable.

This may sound like a large order for a book to fill, but a little research would illustrate the fact that most great men have been activated to succeed by a number of books. In our culture, probably the best example is that of Abraham Lincoln reading by the flickering light of the open hearth.

Television plays a large part in today's life, but, in the main, dreams are still kindled by books. Most people would not have it otherwise, for television (with some exceptions) is a medium of entertainment, while books remain the chief source of knowledge. Even the professors who give lecture courses learned the bulk of their knowledge from books.

The listing of books in this catalog is representative but it still does not encompass the vast number of volumes you may obtain through the Wilshire Book Company.

Some of you may already have a reading program, in which case we will aid you to the utmost in procuring the material you wish.

Those of you who are casting around for a self-improvement program may probably appreciate some help in building a library tailored to fit your hopes and ambitions. If so, we are always available to aid you instantly.

Many readers have asked if they could call on us personally while visiting Los Angeles and Hollywood. The answer is yes. I and my staff will be delighted to show you every book in the catalog and many more unlisted for lack of space and because this is a specialized book service. You can "browse" to your heart's content.

Please consider this a personal invitation of mine to meet and talk with you whenever you visit this city.

Telephone: 875-1711

Send Orders to:

MELVIN POWERS
12015 Sherman Road, No. Hollywood, California 91605

Send 25c for this unique catalog of books.

Melvin Powers
SELF-IMPROVEMENT
LIBRARY

ASTROLOGY

ASTROLOGY: A FASCINATING HISTORY *P. Naylor*	2.00
ASTROLOGY: HOW TO CHART YOUR HOROSCOPE *Max Heindel*	2.00
ASTROLOGY: YOUR PERSONAL SUN-SIGN GUIDE *Beatrice Ryder*	3.00
ASTROLOGY FOR EVERYDAY LIVING *Janet Harris*	2.00
ASTROLOGY MADE EASY *Astarte*	2.00
ASTROLOGY MADE PRACTICAL *Alexandra Kayhle*	2.00
ASTROLOGY, ROMANCE, YOU AND THE STARS *Anthony Norvell*	3.00
MY WORLD OF ASTROLOGY *Sydney Omarr*	4.00
THOUGHT DIAL *Sydney Omarr*	3.00
ZODIAC REVEALED *Rupert Gleadow*	2.00

BRIDGE, POKER & GAMBLING

ADVANCED POKER STRATEGY & WINNING PLAY *A. D. Livingston*	3.00
BRIDGE BIDDING MADE EASY *Edwin Kantar*	5.00
BRIDGE CONVENTIONS *Edwin Kantar*	4.00
COMPLETE DEFENSIVE BRIDGE PLAY *Edwin B. Kantar*	10.00
HOW TO IMPROVE YOUR BRIDGE *Alfred Sheinwold*	2.00
HOW TO WIN AT DICE GAMES *Skip Frey*	2.00
HOW TO WIN AT POKER *Terence Reese & Anthony T. Watkins*	2.00
INTRODUCTION TO DEFENDER'S PLAY *Edwin B. Kantar*	3.00
SECRETS OF WINNING POKER *George S. Coffin*	3.00
TEST YOUR BRIDGE PLAY *Edwin B. Kantar*	3.00
WINNING AT 21 — An Expert's Guide *John Archer*	3.00
WINNING POKER SYSTEMS *Norman Zadeh*	3.00

BUSINESS STUDY & REFERENCE

CONVERSATION MADE EASY *Elliot Russell*	2.00
EXAM SECRET *Dennis B. Jackson*	2.00
FIX-IT BOOK *Arthur Symons*	2.00
HOW TO DEVELOP A BETTER SPEAKING VOICE *M. Hellier*	2.00
HOW TO MAKE A FORTUNE IN REAL ESTATE *Albert Winnikoff*	3.00
HOW TO MAKE MONEY IN REAL ESTATE *Stanley L. McMichael*	2.00
INCREASE YOUR LEARNING POWER *Geoffrey A. Dudley*	2.00
MAGIC OF NUMBERS *Robert Tocquet*	2.00
PRACTICAL GUIDE TO BETTER CONCENTRATION *Melvin Powers*	2.00
PRACTICAL GUIDE TO PUBLIC SPEAKING *Maurice Forley*	2.00
7 DAYS TO FASTER READING *William S. Schaill*	2.00
SONGWRITERS RHYMING DICTIONARY *Jane Shaw Whitfield*	4.00
SPELLING MADE EASY *Lester D. Basch & Dr. Milton Finkelstein*	2.00
STUDENT'S GUIDE TO BETTER GRADES *J. A. Rickard*	2.00
TEST YOURSELF — Find Your Hidden Talent *Jack Shafer*	2.00
YOUR WILL & WHAT TO DO ABOUT IT *Attorney Samuel G. Kling*	3.00

CHESS & CHECKERS

BEGINNER'S GUIDE TO WINNING CHESS *Fred Reinfeld*	2.00
BETTER CHESS — How to Play *Fred Reinfeld*	2.00
CHECKERS MADE EASY *Tom Wiswell*	2.00
CHESS IN TEN EASY LESSONS *Larry Evans*	2.00
CHESS MADE EASY *Milton L. Hanauer*	2.00
CHESS MASTERY — A New Approach *Fred Reinfeld*	2.00

_____IMPOTENCE & FRIGIDITY *Edwin W. Hirsch, M.D.* 3.00
_____SEX WITHOUT GUILT *Albert Ellis, Ph.D.* 2.00
_____SEXUALLY ADEQUATE MALE *Frank S. Caprio, M.D.* 3.00

METAPHYSICS & OCCULT

_____BOOK OF TALISMANS, AMULETS & ZODIACAL GEMS *William Pavitt* 3.00
_____CONCENTRATION—A Guide to Mental Mastery *Mouni Sadhu* 3.00
_____DREAMS & OMENS REVEALED *Fred Gettings* 2.00
_____EXTRASENSORY PERCEPTION *Simeon Edmunds* 2.00
_____EXTRA-TERRESTRIAL INTELLIGENCE—The First Encounter 6.00
_____FORTUNE TELLING WITH CARDS *P. Foli* 2.00
_____HANDWRITING ANALYSIS MADE EASY *John Marley* 2.00
_____HANDWRITING TELLS *Nadya Olyanova* 3.00
_____HOW TO UNDERSTAND YOUR DREAMS *Geoffrey A. Dudley* 2.00
_____ILLUSTRATED YOGA *William Zorn* 3.00
_____IN DAYS OF GREAT PEACE *Mouni Sadhu* 3.00
_____KING SOLOMON'S TEMPLE IN THE MASONIC TRADITION *Alex Horne* 5.00
_____MAGICIAN — His training and work *W. E. Butler* 2.00
_____MEDITATION *Mouni Sadhu* 3.00
_____MODERN NUMEROLOGY *Morris C. Goodman* 2.00
_____NUMEROLOGY—ITS FACTS AND SECRETS *Ariel Yvon Taylor* 2.00
_____PALMISTRY MADE EASY *Fred Gettings* 2.00
_____PALMISTRY MADE PRACTICAL *Elizabeth Daniels Squire* 3.00
_____PALMISTRY SECRETS REVEALED *Henry Frith* 2.00
_____PRACTICAL YOGA *Ernest Wood* 3.00
_____PROPHECY IN OUR TIME *Martin Ebon* 2.50
_____PSYCHOLOGY OF HANDWRITING *Nadya Olyanova* 3.00
_____SEEING INTO THE FUTURE *Harvey Day* 2.00
_____SUPERSTITION — Are you superstitious? *Eric Maple* 2.00
_____TAROT *Mouni Sadhu* 4.00
_____TAROT OF THE BOHEMIANS *Papus* 3.00
_____TEST YOUR ESP *Martin Ebon* 2.00
_____WAYS TO SELF-REALIZATION *Mouni Sadhu* 3.00
_____WITCHCRAFT, MAGIC & OCCULTISM—A Fascinating History *W. B. Crow* 3.00
_____WITCHCRAFT — THE SIXTH SENSE *Justine Glass* 2.00
_____WORLD OF PSYCHIC RESEARCH *Hereward Carrington* 2.00
_____YOU CAN ANALYZE HANDWRITING *Robert Holder* 2.00

SELF-HELP & INSPIRATIONAL

_____CYBERNETICS WITHIN US *Y. Saparina* 3.00
_____DAILY POWER FOR JOYFUL LIVING *Dr. Donald Curtis* 2.00
_____DOCTOR PSYCHO-CYBERNETICS *Maxwell Maltz, M.D.* 3.00
_____DYNAMIC THINKING *Melvin Powers* 1.00
_____GREATEST POWER IN THE UNIVERSE *U. S. Andersen* 4.00
_____GROW RICH WHILE YOU SLEEP *Ben Sweetland* 2.00
_____GROWTH THROUGH REASON *Albert Ellis, Ph.D.* 3.00
_____GUIDE TO DEVELOPING YOUR POTENTIAL *Herbert A. Otto, Ph.D.* 3.00
_____GUIDE TO LIVING IN BALANCE *Frank S. Caprio, M.D.* 2.00
_____HELPING YOURSELF WITH APPLIED PSYCHOLOGY *R. Henderson* 2.00
_____HELPING YOURSELF WITH PSYCHIATRY *Frank S. Caprio, M.D.* 2.00
_____HOW TO ATTRACT GOOD LUCK *A. H. Z. Carr* 2.00
_____HOW TO CONTROL YOUR DESTINY *Norvell* 3.00
_____HOW TO DEVELOP A WINNING PERSONALITY *Martin Panzer* 3.00
_____HOW TO DEVELOP AN EXCEPTIONAL MEMORY *Young & Gibson* 3.00
_____HOW TO OVERCOME YOUR FEARS *M. P. Leahy, M.D.* 2.00
_____HOW YOU CAN HAVE CONFIDENCE AND POWER *Les Giblin* 3.00
_____HUMAN PROBLEMS & HOW TO SOLVE THEM *Dr. Donald Curtis* 3.00
_____I CAN *Ben Sweetland* 3.00
_____I WILL *Ben Sweetland* 3.00
_____LEFT-HANDED PEOPLE *Michael Barsley* 3.00
_____MAGIC IN YOUR MIND *U. S. Andersen* 3.00
_____MAGIC OF THINKING BIG *Dr. David J. Schwartz* 2.00
_____MAGIC POWER OF YOUR MIND *Walter M. Germain* 3.00
_____MENTAL POWER THRU SLEEP SUGGESTION *Melvin Powers* 1.00

_____ NEW GUIDE TO RATIONAL LIVING *Albert Ellis, Ph.D. - R. Harper, Ph.D.* 3.00
_____ OUR TROUBLED SELVES *Dr. Allan Fromme* 3.00
_____ PRACTICAL GUIDE TO SUCCESS & POPULARITY *C. W. Bailey* 2.00
_____ PSYCHO-CYBERNETICS *Maxwell Maltz, M.D.* 2.00
_____ SCIENCE OF MIND IN DAILY LIVING *Dr. Donald Curtis* 2.00
_____ SECRET POWER OF THE PYRAMIDS *U. S. Andersen* 4.00
_____ SECRET OF SECRETS *U. S. Andersen* 4.00
_____ STUTTERING AND WHAT YOU CAN DO ABOUT IT *W. Johnson, Ph.D.* 2.00
_____ SUCCESS-CYBERNETICS *U. S. Andersen* 3.00
_____ 10 DAYS TO A GREAT NEW LIFE *William E. Edwards* 3.00
_____ THINK AND GROW RICH *Napoleon Hill* 3.00
_____ THREE MAGIC WORDS *U. S. Andersen* 3.00
_____ TREASURY OF THE ART OF LIVING *Sidney S. Greenberg* 3.00
_____ YOU ARE NOT THE TARGET *Laura Huxley* 3.00
_____ YOUR SUBCONSCIOUS POWER *Charles M. Simmons* 3.00
_____ YOUR THOUGHTS CAN CHANGE YOUR LIFE *Dr. Donald Curtis* 3.00

SPORTS

_____ ARCHERY — An Expert's Guide *Don Stamp* 2.00
_____ BICYCLING FOR FUN AND GOOD HEALTH *Kenneth E. Luther* 2.00
_____ BILLIARDS—Pocket • Carom • Three Cushion *Clive Cottingham, Jr.* 2.00
_____ CAMPING-OUT 101 Ideas & Activities *Bruno Knobel* 2.00
_____ COMPLETE GUIDE TO FISHING *Vlad Evanoff* 2.00
_____ HOW TO WIN AT POCKET BILLIARDS *Edward D. Knuchell* 3.00
_____ LEARNING & TEACHING SOCCER SKILLS *Eric Worthington* 3.00
_____ MOTORCYCLING FOR BEGINNERS *I. G. Edmonds* 2.00
_____ PRACTICAL BOATING *W. S. Kals* 3.00
_____ SECRET OF BOWLING STRIKES *Dawson Taylor* 2.00
_____ SECRET OF PERFECT PUTTING *Horton Smith & Dawson Taylor* 2.00
_____ SECRET WHY FISH BITE *James Westman* 2.00
_____ SKIER'S POCKET BOOK *Otti Wiedman* (4¼″ x 6″) 2.50
_____ SOCCER—The game & how to play it *Gary Rosenthal* 2.00
_____ TABLE TENNIS MADE EASY *Johnny Leach* 2.00

TENNIS LOVERS' LIBRARY

_____ BEGINNER'S GUIDE TO WINNING TENNIS *Helen Hull Jacobs* 2.00
_____ HOW TO BEAT BETTER TENNIS PLAYERS *Loring Fiske* 3.00
_____ HOW TO IMPROVE YOUR TENNIS—Style, Strategy & Analysis *C. Wilson* 2.00
_____ INSIDE TENNIS — Techniques of Winning *Jim Leighton* 3.00
_____ PLAY TENNIS WITH ROSEWALL *Ken Rosewall* 2.00
_____ PSYCH YOURSELF TO BETTER TENNIS *Dr. Walter A. Luszki* 2.00
_____ SUCCESSFUL TENNIS *Neale Fraser* 2.00
_____ TENNIS FOR BEGINNERS *Dr. H. A. Murray* 2.00
_____ TENNIS MADE EASY *Joel Brecheen* 2.00
_____ WEEKEND TENNIS—How to have fun & win at the same time *Bill Talbert* 2.00
_____ WINNING WITH PERCENTAGE TENNIS *Jack Lowe* 2.00
An Expert's Guide to Smart Court Strategy & Technique

WILSHIRE MINIATURE LIBRARY (4¼″ x 6″ in full color)

_____ BUTTERFLIES 2.50
_____ LIPIZZANERS & THE SPANISH RIDING SCHOOL 2.50
_____ SKIER'S POCKET BOOK 2.50

WILSHIRE PET LIBRARY

_____ DOG OBEDIENCE TRAINING *Gust Kessopulos* 3.00
_____ DOG TRAINING MADE EASY & FUN *John W. Kellogg* 2.00
_____ HOW TO BRING UP YOUR PET DOG *Kurt Unkelbach* 2.00
_____ HOW TO RAISE & TRAIN YOUR PUPPY *Jeff Griffen* 2.00
_____ PIGEONS: HOW TO RAISE & TRAIN THEM *William H. Allen, Jr.* 2.00

The books listed above can be obtained from your book dealer or directly from Melvin Powers. When ordering, please remit 25c per book postage & handling. Send 25c for our illustrated catalog of self-improvement books.

Melvin Powers

12015 Sherman Road, No. Hollywood, California 91605

NOTES

NOTES

NOTES